Soul,
Sweat
and
Survival
on the
Pacific Crest Trail

Bob Holtel

Bittersweet Publishing Company
Livermore, California

Front cover: Author on Chikamin Ridge in Washington's Cascades. Photo by Lee Freeman.

Rear cover: Photo by Lee Freeman.

Parts of this book have previously been copyrighted: p.129. © 1987 The Mountaineers. Quoted with permission of the publisher from *Journey On The Crest* by Cindy Ross; p.145. © 1976 Alfred A. Knopf. Quoted with permission of the publisher from *Reflections From The North Country* by Sigurd Olson.

Library of Congress Catalog Card Number: 93-74046
International Standard Book Number: 0-931255-07-4

Published by Bittersweet Publishing Company
Post Office Box 1211, Livermore, California 94551

Printed in the United States of America on recycled paper.

To

Rich Dinges

Ron Flowers

Herman Kuhn

three special human beings

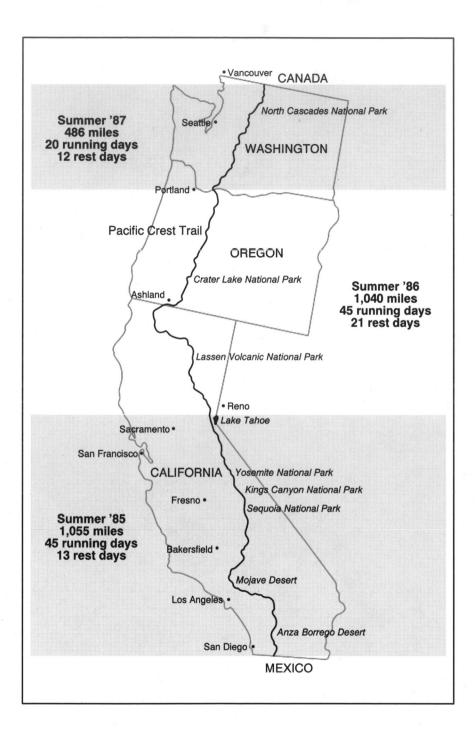

Contents

Author above Park Lakes Basin   by Lee Freeman

Acknowledgments

I am amazed at the time and compassion each dedicated volunteer has given to making my dream a reality. The run and this book were, in large part, the result of a huge supporting cast. I will never forget each and every one of them.

This book would not have been possible without the invaluable expertise of Bonnie Darves and A. D. Doug Emerson who gave special attention to its content and format.

My dedicated manuscript typist, Cheryl Frankosky, put in many hours above and beyond the call.

I am eternally grateful to running companion, John Stewart (a chief editor for the *Los Angeles Times*), and Paul Silva (former editor of my hometown newspaper), for their early critiques and positive encouragement.

Michael Powe greatly assisted with intricate computer-drawn maps and altitude charts.

Brian Gauthier, one of my former students and a professional editor, added some fine-tuning.

I extend my utmost appreciation to my two literary bookends: Kenny Moore (senior editor for *Sports Illustrated*) for the Introduction to this book, along with critical commentary along the way; and Joe Henderson (West Coast editor for *Runner's World*) for the Epilogue, as well as colorful chapter subheading ideas.

My heartfelt gratitude to Mike Dirham for the overall editing, with special emphasis on transition flow and clarity of philosophical passages. The creative illustrations throughout the text are just one of his many incredible talents. They inject episodes of raw humor into a serious and spiritual journey.

Special thanks to my computer expert, Bob Schratz, for putting all the pieces together into the draft that I needed in my search for a publisher, and for making my goal his goal.

My publisher, Marcus Libkind, has proven to be highly disciplined, with a keen eye for intrinsic detail. Working with Marcus would be a pleasure for any writer.

There were also those who realized that my journey was not meant to be a self-centered gesture, but rather a personal learning experience and a lesson for others. These people and companies, Dr. John Pagliano, Dr. Bruce Letvin, Lon Clearwaters, Michelle Icaza, Powerfood, Bodyfuel, New Balance, Patagonia, Second Sole, and Hostelhaus provided equipment and financial support for my odyssey.

Plaudits to my daughter, Linda, for planning a surprise homecoming celebration, and to my son, Michael, for his moral support throughout the run.

My mom and dad carve a special niche with their unflagging inspiration. My sincere thanks to them for tolerating my simple and often transitory lifestyle.

And last but not least I would like to express my sincere appreciation to the vast supporting cast who enthusiastically and unselfishly gave their free time and an all-out effort to make this enduro possible. They paced me, they shuttled my gear, they placed caches at strategic locations, they met me at various locations along the trail with fresh supplies and human warmth, they cooked hot meals for me, they supplied me with shelter, and they make tears come to my eyes when I think of all they have done for me. So it is fitting that your names are placed on this "Honor Roll."

John and Janice Anderson
Jon Anderson
Carlos Arellanes
Ernie Baker
Janet and Martin Balding
Del Beaudoin
Amie Beisel
Gary and Kate Belanger
Jerry Blinn
Maurie Bosquet
Dave Buckner
Bob and Patti Carpenter
Steve "Slick" and Kim Chapman
Mary Beth Cook
John and Shirley Cosgrove
Don and Robin Crowell
Rich "Steamroller" Dinges
Jim Drake
John and Kitty Emig
Rick and Donna Fay
Lee Freeman
Tom Fish
Robert and Gayle Frickel
Chuck and Nancy Giardini
Jim and Cheri Girod
Larry Goodman and friend Gretchen
Terry and Marilynn Grant
Ken Hamada
Thor Hanson
Judy and Wayne Harpel
Chris Hawk
Barry "Baz" Hawley
Fred and Velma Hermann
Ted Hill
Kent and Ann Holder
Hans Holtz
Judy Ikenberry

Larry and Moe Jackson
Bruce Johnson
Jay and Kay Jones
Milt Kenney
T. J. "Running Feather" Key
Danny Kessler
Jim and Tina King
Lew and Joanna Knickerbocker
Steve Knipper
Steve Kohler
Willard and Jean Krick
Tim Lauridsen
Kip and Jody Leonard
Boyd Levet
Jan Levet
Carl Long
Dario Malengo
Rick Maltin
Bruce Mauldin
Brian McBean
Kevin McCready
"Buffalo Bill" McDermott
Mike McMahon
Russ Melanson
John Middleton
Kenny Moore
Court and Janis Mumford
Mitch Regal
Jack Slater
Jim Taylor and three friends
Nancy Taylor
Chips Thompson
Jose Torres
Rob Volkenand
Lary Webster
Hal Winton
Ted Zimbelman

Introduction

We who know him had little doubt that Bob Holtel would successfully complete the first ever run from Mexico to Canada over the Pacific Crest Trail. No one has ever been able to wear him out. But we were intensely curious about the manuscript he would produce.

You see, Holtel, in person, is terse. An adjective a week, that's all he uses. Just as he excluded even a sleeping bag from the gear that had to keep him alive over high mountain passes, he stripped his speech down to the pith. Sometimes, after the style of the West Torrance High School kids he taught and coached, he reduces words to initials. Thus his highest praise is a dry "N.T.S." — not too shabby. Holtel reads by underlining a work's bedrock phrases. For him the most obscure, rambling book yields an obsidian-hard moral order. He does not tell stories as much as recite lists. What did he see during the Western States 100-Miler? "Six waterfalls, 11 lakes, 16 rattlers, 37 deer, etc." Rhythmic and heartfelt, but lists.

Yet his voice, with a clipped hint of John Wayne in it, can be compelling. He makes tone take the place of language. He talks to us like dogs. His Pacific Crest Trail adventure, then, seemed one of a harsh man seeking the ultimate harshness.

By now you're wondering too. What kind of a book was this guy going to write?

Of course it would be a determined one. He sweated over his first draft as he did across the Mojave. He wanted to do what he had never done before. He wanted to find language to bear all he had experienced. He wrote a crazily complex narrative, so dense with supercharged prose that the upper McKenzie lava fields were easier to get through. This had not been created by a secret Holtel that none of us had suspected. He had just run up against the limits of words. Under the full weight of his experience, his language cracked and buckled.

What he wanted to do could not be done. Literature can't put 30 miles of dusty trail into a reader's quadriceps. It can't recreate the wild force of a restorative beer hitting a near-dead system. It can't induce the trance of sleep in alpine air, the cleanliness of a spirit washed by a day-long jarring effort.

No, writing simply instills images in the reader's mind. In his second draft, Holtel had to be content with guiding our imaginings. This is what it was LIKE, not what it was. For those as unhappy with that as he is, Holtel offers a five-hour run over wrenching switchbacks with him every Saturday.

Reading his extraordinary story, it becomes clear that harshness is Holtel's means to virtue. His life of extreme physical effort makes everything false or pretentious simply evaporate. What is left is the simple and the good. That is N.T.S. in any man's book.

There. You're introduced, although it would be a lie to say you are prepared. Who among us is prepared for a man to get up and run 2,600 miles over the mountains?

Kenny Moore
Senior Writer for Sports Illustrated[1]
and Former Olympic Marathoner
December 30, 1988

---

[1] Organization given for identification only.

Author concentrating while running in High Sierra   by Robert Frickel

1 Could It Be Done? _____

Far better it is to dare mighty things, to win glorious triumphs, even though checkered by failure, than to take rank with those poor spirits who neither enjoy much nor suffer much, because they live in the gray twilight that knows not victory or defeat.

— Theodore Roosevelt

A flash storm hurls huge hailstones at us, and the lightning is so fierce and close that it rattles the ground beneath us. The hail stings our cheeks and burns our backs, and then builds up under us, making some of the smooth rocks slippery.

The graying sky is punctuated by blue flashes of terror — our adrenalin is pumping. In a hectic sprint we make a quick thrust toward lower and friendlier territory. Body hair stands on end as we're surrounded by electrical currents that resemble the drone of insects. I entertain the idea of tossing anything metallic.

Two well-disguised rattlers cross the trail. The morning has been so intense that it's difficult to muster yet another surge of adrenalin, but my heart pounds as we detour, chilling with trepidation. I steal another glance at the rattlers, marveling at how closely they match the terrain. I'm fortunate I have a pacer in case of a mishap. What I cannot say is expressed by the reverberating echoes of the storm in the canyons, which ricochet like gun shots. Cold, oxygen-depleted air irritates my already slightly sore throat.

We descend with intense concentration, our mental controls locked on automatic pilot. Each breath strains my lungs to capacity. Time seems to slip away. I find my already fragile grasp on reality rapidly dissolving. A brightly painted rainbow flickers over a knife-edge ridge, suffusing the land with an uncanny peace. Nonetheless, my discomfort cannot be ignored, and I feel like I'm running a marathon with a plastic bag over my head.

Am I doing this run for recognition or am I avoiding responsibility? Or, could I be trying to find a slot outside the real world where my wilderness mentality will be more acceptable?

It is my ninth day north from the border. During these anxious moments I contemplate how it all began.

The Run

This journey was a dream of simplicity, of pitting personal strength against the incalculable strength of Mother Nature. Not to conquer her, but rather to experience her from the closest vantage point allowed our species:

one on one. However, before I planted that first footstrike, there were many times when my doubt outweighed my excitement — moments of raw fear of the thousands of miles that lay before me — times when the waking consideration of the dangers I would face overwhelmed me.

On a hot summer morning just after daybreak, not long after my 53rd birthday, I will begin this trail run to fulfill a goal conceived many years ago — to run the Pacific Crest National Scenic Trail from the Mexican to the Canadian border.

No one has ever done this. I realize I will be the first. It is a long way — 2,581 miles — not counting side trips to resupply. The distance will escalate by 57 miles three years later. New trail usually combines less gradient with slightly greater convolutions.

My incredibly arduous itinerary entails running, on the average, just under a marathon a day. Much of it will involve steep, rocky trails with precarious footing through oxygen-starved, spectacular mountain ranges.

Other parts of the trail are desolate. I will travel more than a week through the God forsaken deserts of Southern California, with their searing heat, seeing many more animals than people.

I am eager to make my way to Canada. I want to alleviate my fear of the unknown and turn it into a lifelong memory. This means turning my back on all that was warm and secure on the home front. I will become an uncertain intruder in an unfamiliar territory — a running animal flashing past the flora and fauna of all the ecological life zones. The dream is not just exciting. It is a live, passionate, breathing little creature that sits on my shoulder and whispers in my ear every hour of every day. But dreams don't come true easily. I started preparing in 1980, five years before taking my first step northward.

The myriad of meticulous details — thorough map study, locating food caches, assuring fresh shoes were available, arranging for human support in the dangerously remote areas — threaten to prevent me from making it a reality. My determination, perseverance, and patience are severely taxed from the onset, but I persist and on the 10th of July, 1985, I kick the fence at the Mexico-United States border.

I am not aware that undertaking this run will ultimately have more impact on my life than any other single thing I could conceivably do. In redefining my physical limitations, I will achieve a spiritual awareness I'd never even considered. The world I leave behind in 1985 will never be the same, at least in the sense that I can never again view it in the exact same way. Any past habitual ruts I have allowed myself to succumb to will be forever challenged and become pointless as I embrace the journey.

Most grueling will be the daily personal struggle — masochistic 12-hour days, fierce storms, bone-numbing cold. In addition I will encounter other forms of life whose "homes" I will trespass in my travels.

For basic survival, I will have to locate approximately 1,300 quarts of potable water before touching Canadian soil.

Crucial supplies, occasional support teams, and pacers are contingent upon being at specified places at specific times. If only to keep from causing alarm, I have to adhere to a schedule that offers limited flexibility. Thus, on the days when my calves feel like old, splintered wood and my hips like mortar and pestle, I take off at dawn anyway — even if that dawn brings rain, thunder, and lightning, or it follows a completely sleepless night.

My outfit consists of nylon shorts, running shoes, gloves, a wool hat, a visor, a Gore-Tex windbreaker, rain pants, several long sleeve polypropylene shirts, and a trashbag raincoat. It will be a meager covering when I reach the Washington Cascades in the summer of '87.

Why?

RISK

To reach out is to risk involvement
To expose feelings is to risk exposing your true self
To place your ideas, your dreams before the crowd is to
risk their loss
To love is to risk not being loved in return
To live is to risk dying
To hope is to risk despair
To try is to risk failure
But risks must be taken because the greatest hazard in life
is to risk nothing
The person who risks nothing, does nothing, has nothing,
is nothing
He may avoid suffering and sorrow but he simply cannot
learn, feel, change, grow, love, live . . .
Chained by his certitudes, he is a slave
He has forfeited freedom
Only a person who risks is free

— Anonymous

Running the Pacific Crest Trail from Mexico to Canada culminates a running career that began in high school. I have coached long distance athletes for thirty years and have competed in races on four continents.

Wilderness running is different, though. After four decades of backpacking and trekking along mountaintops and through deserts, I feel I know the distinction. It is natural for me to look for new worlds to conquer.

A wilderness adventure of this magnitude — with only the contents of a 15-pound fanny pack as my primary life support system — will put me face to face with enough risk to transcend all my past achievements. This risk, both the controlled and the uncontrolled variety, will be greater than on any runs I have ever experienced before. I fall in love with the idea and the excitement its danger entails. I embrace it!

In real life, people can be divided into three groups:

> *Those who make things happen, those who watch things happen, and those who wonder what happened.*

— John W. Newbern

I voraciously devour the sparse literature on adventure running.

The Tarahumara Indians of Mexico immediately come to mind. Fueled by a corn-based, fermented brew, they run several hundred miles over a period of days, herding animals while kicking a small wooden ball. Almost all the participants are under 35 and staggering drunk for much of the duration. It is part of their religion.

The longest runs completed to date for the most part take place on easily accessible roads. Such runs offer more than a modicum of luxury afforded by the knowledge that along the way there will be creature comforts. That is why, perhaps, the run of the Pacific Crest Trail in its entirety, from the Mexican to the Canadian border, has never been attempted.

Chikamin Ridge in Washington   by Lee Freeman

I knew I would never enjoy running across the country on Interstate 80, with 18-wheelers boring down on me at 70 miles per hour, not to mention the trail of exhaust fumes, the knee-jarring surfaces, and especially the ultimate boredom of paralleling our modern transportation arteries.

Runner Jay Birmingham, among others, once covered the 146 miles from the lowest to highest elevations in the continental United States — Death Valley to Mt. Whitney. In his subsequent account of his trek, *The Longest Day*, he wrote four words inside the front cover that struck home: DREAM, PREPARE, ENDURE, ACHIEVE!

I drink in all the inspiration I can find, and as July 1985 gets closer, I begin to wake in the night, filled with anxiety about the enormity of the challenge. The potential disasters on this run make the weekend group runs sponsored by running clubs look like Sunday school picnics.

Whatever other reasons I might find to avoid the challenge, I cannot abandon it just because it is too long or too difficult. As I grow more aware of how brief our time is in this world, personal mortality smacks me square in the eyeball. From these long, free moments of dream, this run takes up permanent residence within my craving bowels.

I have a gut-level desire to run "one-with-nature" for a sustained time. I posture myself as an intrepid pioneer earning passage through hard, clean toil. I will self-propel a scantily clad running body over 100 high mountain passes, gaps, and summits in all weather conditions. I will have to extract from myself an incomprehensible daily quotient of punishing discomfort, hopefully with minimal complaint.

How

The mind-boggling, logistical nightmare of spending over five months on a trail at high altitude, with no more than 15 pounds of gear at any point, terrifies me. Unlike the backpacker's pack, stuffed with tent, sleeping bag, cooking gear, and other amenities of civilization, my entire lifeline will be in the zippered pockets of one "fanny pack." I studiously research ultralight camping to learn how to keep paraphernalia to the basic minimum. With every ounce counting, even the toothbrush handle must go.

I will pre-mail the maximum number of supply packages feasible to various post offices in small towns and tiny resorts located near the trail. These care-caches primarily contain high energy bars, trail mix, dried fruit, granola, electrolyte powder, rice cakes, crackers, and just about anything else compact that does not require cooking. It will be a never ending battle to keep my weight up and stay clean.

I will also carry or mail ahead water purification tablets, matches and fire starter, a snake bite kit, an ankle brace, traveler's checks (for hot meals on rest days), sunscreen, repellent, lip ice, a tiny flashlight (with extra bulb and batteries), skin lotion, toilet paper, maps, compass, aspirin, pen, pad, running shoes with special inserts, and other minimal essentials. I will survive with a tiny bivy sack and sleeping bag liner each night.

I schedule my food drops three to four days apart to keep the fanny pack from feeling like lead or bursting a seam. This depends largely on the proximity of my supply center and the ease of getting there. Unforeseen delays due to unseasonable weather could force me to miss several meals.

Food alone will average two pounds per day. I can not expect to find nutritious, lightweight trail items at small general stores. When you do find them, prices can be exorbitant.

Essentials cover the entire front room floor for weeks. No part of the rug is visible. I write to various Pacific Crest Trail organizations for strategic post office locations. I send the latter self-addressed, stamped cards with a note requesting the days and times they are open. I have to plan the number of travel days between zones, take weekends into consideration, and allow extra time for boxes to get to isolated areas.

I meticulously divide the vast accumulation of goodies into individual meal portions, funnel them into over two hundred plastic Ziploc bags, and pack everything in thirty caches pre-addressed to thirty post offices. I present them to fifteen close friends and neighbors. I have to predetermine an exact mailing date for each as well as my expected arrival time. Whew!

I am so well prepared through topographical map scrutiny that I know the location of every stream crossing and side trail before I get there.

I believe I am sufficiently toughened; my apprenticeship includes 123,000 running miles divided among 128 marathons (26.2 miles), thirty-six 50-mile trail races, four 100-mile enduros, and a couple of Great Hawaiian footraces. I have run extensively in the Grand Canyon, New Zealand, Europe, and in over 100 state parks and national forests. Despite this, the thought of running the trail, virtually alone and at the mercy of the elements, often overwhelms me.

Two friends and I had recently run the John Muir Trail from Mt. Whitney to Yosemite Valley. We averaged slightly under a marathon a day on each of the nine days. At least two-thirds of the terrain is over 9,000 feet. Even at 53, my body is probably as finely tuned as it can be; I am physically prepared.

I also know that my puppy "Blazer" will have to stay at home. He has been my running companion for numerous trail miles. Even if back-country regulations would permit it, the inevitable paw soreness and ever-present potential for injury make it unfeasible. Also, Blazer and snakes and bears don't mix.

Initially, I keep my plans to myself. I know my friends will think I am nuts. Being by nature one who detests crowds and noise, I seek to stand tall on my own and not burden others with a concept that will surely dredge up their own anxieties. However, when I let my secret out they appreciate the probability for mishaps and the hazards involved.

I know that the bare necessities in the fanny pack, dictated by weight, space, and versatility, will knead and punch my buttocks and hips over the 2,600 miles. After you complete a few 50-mile runs you even think about how you can stop the jostling of a band-aid over a raw blister.

I will have to travel up and down almost one-half million feet. From the lowest point, the Columbia River Gorge at 170 feet, to the uppermost point, Forester Pass at 13,180 feet, measures approximately two and

Contemplating a roaring stream crossing   by Lee Freeman

one-half vertical miles. The most isolated parts of the run include the Anza Borrego and Mojave deserts. The steepest and highest areas cover the Sierra Nevada passes near Mt. Whitney.

About 300 miles of the trail is relatively flat. The remaining 2,300 miles have grades up to 15%. The grades on the freeways seldom go above 10%. That one-half million feet calculates out to around 100 miles, roughly fifty miles up and fifty miles down. Now think a minute — how many people take the escalator up to the third floor and back down again? That's about a 100-foot round trip. You would have to do that over 4,000 times without the escalator if you ran the Pacific Crest Trail's cumulative gradient.

In the late 70's and early 80's, I made my way to different locations on this National Scenic Trail, running three-day segments as precursors. Many parts of the trail were badly overgrown. Mileage signs had been vandalized by shooters, partially eaten by bears, or demolished by lightning. Unmarked junctions led me on frustrating wrong routes. I got to know some of the worst sections. I learned a lot.

The solitude and mystical allure of these mountain trails compelled me. In the duel taking place in my head, the solo adventurer somewhat vanquishes his fearful opponent: the guy who is happy with group runs, short runs, and the acceptability of being an in-member of an in-group of runners.

The Pacific Crest Trail is covered with snow and ice in the winter months. This necessitates dividing the run into three summer segments. The first will negotiate 1,055 trail miles from the wire fence at Campo on the Mexican border to Donner Pass in the Sierra. I'll complete that section in 58 days, utilizing 45 running days and 13 rest days (for recuperation and resupply). In this first "installment," I will traverse thirty mountain passes, seventeen of them at altitudes above 9,000 feet. Of those, three are over 12,000 feet.

The second leg spans from Donner Pass to the Columbia River Gorge, a distance of 1,040 miles. I will complete this segment in 66 days with a running to rest ratio similar to the first summer. This will prove to be the roughest summer because I'll be virtually alone 75% of the time. I have to run side trails to rural hamlets and lake resorts to resupply. It will be by far the loneliest. I will encounter the most rattlers and bears but the least number of mountain passes — only 15.

The finale encompasses the comparatively short distance of 486 miles over 32 days — 20 for running and 12 for recovery. It sounds like a rather nonchalant run compared to the other two segments, but I knew it would not be. There are almost no towns within remote proximity of the Pacific Crest Trail in Washington. Storms are frequent, vehement, and sometimes offer no warning. I will traverse 55 mountain passes and gaps.

Summits in Washington over 6,000 feet are generally up around timberline. They harbor the same potentially icy, wind chill conditions as

Trail descent between Deception Lakes and Stevens Pass   by Lee Freeman

10,000-foot passes in California's Sierra. This is because of their northern locale and proximity to endless glaciers.

I turn my energy to finding sponsors, confident that a solo trail run over rugged terrain on the Pacific Crest Trail is a worthy, substantial endeavor and hardly a whimsical escapade. After all, I live in Southern California, the home of more sports, more sporting enthusiasts, more sporting media, and more sporting equipment manufacturers than anywhere else in the world. We spend more on frisbees than the national budgets of several countries in the United Nations. Surely I can find a willing sponsor, I believe, but no. All my initial efforts are unsuccessful. From the volume of weekly rejections I receive, you'd have thought I was applying to medical schools. Major companies will patronize only Olympic athletes. They give "canned" excuses about their tight budgets or promise to wave at me as I pass through their state. Others emit the increasingly familiar: "Call us after you've done it!"

I never give up hope, and a few individuals and companies come through:

Brian Maxwell of Powerfood donates a generous amount of high-energy bars. New Balance, whose shoes I will wear throughout the run, supplies the nine pairs I'll need. Two renowned Southern California podiatrists, John Pagliano and Bruce Letvin, concoct a crucial foot-care survival kit. Bodyfuel provides me ample carbohydrate replacement mix.

I recruit thirty-some running friends to pace me for one or more days each during the first leg. With their support I begin to envision a composite of care and cheering that will propel me on my journey.

I enlist this moral support because there are 25-mile stretches of trail with no potable water. Also, I will be running the driest segments in the summer. Of ongoing concern is the harrowing possibility of a severe ankle twist, a wrenched knee, painful achilles swelling, a serious fall, a venomous snake bite, pus-laden blisters, sudden severe storms, sliding down an icefield in shorts, altitude sickness, giardia, bear confrontations, wind chill, lightning strikes on exposed ridges, hypothermia, and dangerous stream crossings.

Scorching desert temperatures can result in dehydration, cramping, severely blistered lips, chafing, eye redness, and painful sunburn. Dehydration impairs good judgment and occasionally kills.

If I break a hip or femur out there, or rupture an appendix, I am finished. If I die out there while solo running, no one would know where or how for who knows how long.

Lastly, I wonder how I will put a handle on the inevitable stints of overwhelming emotional trauma, loneliness, and depression. I am counting on the physical activity to enhance my mental state.

I find strength in reading and rereading these motivating words by Calvin Coolidge:

Nothing in the world can take the place of persistence.
Talent will not; nothing is more common than unsuccess-
ful men with talent. Genius will not; unrewarded genius
is almost a proverb. Education alone will not; the world
is full of educated derelicts. Persistence and determination
alone are omnipotent.

One friend stokes my fire when he reminds me that "One who follows the crowd gets no farther than its group-imposed limitations. One who sets out alone finds himself in places hardly anyone has been!"

I know there will be a lot of cold ground and lonely hillsides on center stage of my upcoming effort.

A ship is safest in port, but that's not what ships are for. I am eager to launch as I wait for dawn to break on Day Number One of 110 long ones.

Summer of '85
Mexico to Donner Pass

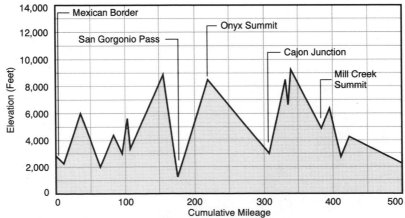

Stretching out at 4:30 a.m. at the Mexican border   by Moe Jackson

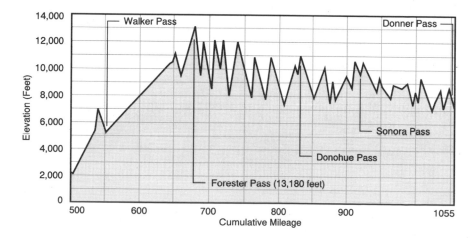

Fresh on the trail one morning   by Robert Krickel

2 A Dry and Lonely Start _____

*We need to know ourselves not only as social and eco-
nomic creatures but as a natural species, as brothers and
sisters of all life, humble participants in mystery. . . . And
any relation of human being to the natural world trans-
lates as personal, spiritual experience. From tame gera-
niums to wild peaks and forests, nature contains me and
I contain it. Going deeply into nature, I find myself. If I
forget to repudiate nature, I myself am lost.*

— Wallace Stegner

Adios, Mexico

Day One - July 10, 1985, 4:30 a.m.   Just below Campo, California, I
stretch by a weather-beaten fence at the Mexican border, fanny pack, sole
companion and life source, snugly girding my waist. A full hour before
daybreak the heat of the previous day can still be felt in the parched earth.
Lifetime friend Moe Jackson, my drop-off support cog, shadows me with
her car headlights for the first mile on an adjacent fire road, and then she
departs. I pummel a pounding heart back into my chest and head north
through the spiny, desolate gullies that bisect an eerie second growth of
regenerating chaparral. Sparse wildlife borders the barely discernible trail
on today's uphill 30-plus-miler.

A few miles later I look for the pesky territorial rattler whose venomous attack the week before traumatized a friend's ankle and put him in ICU
for 48 hours. Through the overgrown stretch north of Cibbets Flat I carry
a long stick and tax my peripheral vision, but do not spot the pugnacious
reptile. Before this journey is over, I will encounter 45 slithering serpents,
some audibly buzzing like an overhead wire junction.

By midafternoon, feeling like a mountain missionary, I surge into
Burndt Rancheria Campground carried on a frisky whirlwind that spins
the tumbleweed into dancing spirals. As a Roman Catholic with knowledge
of the religion's California history, I consider what it must have been like
here for such early explorers as Junipero Serra. On a gimpy leg, he trekked
thousands of miles on foot across the trackless mountains and deserts
planting the seeds of Christianity. What a different type of journey that
was from the one so many people make today where just getting from point
A to point B on crowded freeways is considered an adventure. I cannot
imagine how I weathered the urban wastelands or found the patience to
commute to work in the snarl of heavy traffic.

Just outside the campground, the first of many precious care packages
awaits my arrival. It is provided by Moe's hubby, outstanding ultradis-

tance runner, Tommy Jackson. In three gulps, a good portion of the high energy contents disappear. When the heat dissipates, I treat myself to a leisurely supper of pasta salad and follow the red ribbons in the sky until it becomes a slate for a starlit night.

My bed of hardpacked dirt is softened only by the one-quarter inch thickness of two tiny ensolite pads. A broken sleep follows while I sort out sounds, half listening for rattlers and other predators. Instead, a tiny mouse runs across my face, then trots off to nibble on some leftover trail mix crumbs. After a series of stunts, including double and triple somersaults, tailspins, and nosedives (all on a full stomach!), my visitor, using my chin as a diving board, scurries off into the forest as I nod off to sleep.

Acrobatic mouse   by Mike Dirham

A Disciplined Charge

Day 2 - July 11.   At dawn I pound out another 30-miler through butchered debris and gnarly roots. I am so glad to be done with preparations. I am rid of civilization and all its frustrating constraints. I'm free! I'm organized, and I'm free. The elation I feel after sleeping the first night on the trail is hard to describe. I charge along the trail like I am a kid again, but it is a disciplined charge.

By 10 a.m. I am parched by the searing heat that scorches my shoulders and thighs. Prior to Al Bahr Camp, water has been scarce — now none is available until Pioneer Mail. The trail is signless. My stomach lurches in fear at the thought of worsening thirst and the possibility of losing the trail. The entangled buckthorn whips my calves. Suddenly, a frisky fawn springs to its feet and is gone in a flash. A watchful doe interrupts her nibbling and stretches her neck to check out the intrusion. She hurdles a massive log and leaps down a game trail only to have her speed checked four jumps later by the soft desert sand. I meet her puzzled silence with my own wide grin as I marvel at the little miracles of the wilderness.

The awaited oasis at Chariot Springs doesn't materialize. It is only a trickle, putting me at thimbleful level for the final hour of the day's run.

When a turn in the trail brings Banner Store into view, my audible sigh startles me. Dreamy scents from the tiny resort reach my nostrils. A garden hose shower at the store flushes dirt off my skin as the dust runs down in streams. I squeal like a 6-year-old as I gurgle the abundance and emit a loud grateful sigh. As I cool off, two friends pull up.

San Diego based ultrarunner, Larry Goodman and his sidekick, Gretchen, spring a surprise health food dinner of homemade lasagna and fresh fruit. These peerless flatlanders depart at sundown, and I spend the second night in an open field skirted by sandstone mesas. A half dozen silver-gray fluffy squirrels provide my company. I am especially drawn to a handsome fellow with black, tufted ears and sideburns. Acting as pack leader, he methodically picks his way around the perimeter with silent, cautious movements of his large furry paws.

Day 3 - July 12. Not thrilled by the prospect of repeating the no-water adventure, I take off with an extra four pounds and now tote a full gallon of water in five bottles. The weight's bad enough, but its throttling movement is pure assault to the senses and threatens early fatigue. But I have no choice since I am well over 25 miles from the next water.

It is a hellish 100 degrees. I run through the Anza Borrego Desert at midday in a blinding sandstorm. I can barely peer out between the narrow slits of pebble-blasted eyelids. The camber of the trail aggravates the pain in my calves, and I slow down to accommodate conditions. Each mile feels like three.

I battle the incessant assault by an air force of angry, arrogant flies that whoosh down on me in clusters. Flailing at them, I nearly wrench my right shoulder to keep one especially large bunch from whipping my face.

As the hours pass and the temperature continues to climb, a final swallow from the fifth bottle sets off a bell inside of me. Long, tough, hilly gradients lie ahead. Panic sets in. I am swaying and shaking. My skin is sweatless. My hands are raw and callused from carrying the bottles. My fatigue is absolute. I look down at my cramping calves and quads, and the ground becomes a dance of fuzzy reddish-brown and gray. In my now hallucinatory state, even a buggy quagmire with rainwater remnants holds dreamy appeal.

My bladder aches as if I have to urinate. Nothing comes out when I attempt to initiate a flow. It grows worse each time I negotiate a downhill trail parcel. Several switchbacks later, I pause and squat as my bowels are on fire with more than marginal diarrhea. How can this be? Did I eat some spoiled food on yesterday's side-trail village visit? Did I neglect to allow the iodine tabs to dissolve sufficiently the other day when water sources were scarce? It is all conjecture now as I dream about flushing out an inner network of overworked pipes with Lomotil, granola, and fluids.

The curse returns throughout the day as a multitude of pit stops display unpleasant scents and colors. I warily scrutinize grotesque designs within my own residue. The daily ache of screaming muscles and tendons, temporarily hushed by icy stream dips (if available) and Advil, is expected. This was not!

Fear is like a magnet — it attracts the thing most feared — possible dehydration and renal shutdown. I stoke myself through the remaining miles, chanting my prayers like mantras.

Hard clean discipline pulls and stretches a person. It becomes a journey from the comfortable to the new and untried, from security to challenge.

My macho attempts to show no signs of weakness suddenly strike me as ridiculous. There are no human spectators, and the wildlife have their own survival to deal with. I put all brain conductors in neutral to numb the never-ending twinges from thrashed feet and my abused lower back. I am one whipped hombre when I stagger into Warner Springs in the late afternoon.

I am greeted by locals who had gotten word of a runner "going all the way." After devouring two quarts of apple juice, two boxes of blackberries and six ripe, warm peaches, I began psyching up for dinner. My insatiable appetite is tested by a gourmet enduro that includes: a massive chicken burrito, two cheese enchiladas, two tacos, a chile relleno, six flour tortillas, and a bed of beans and rice — washed down with some dark Dos Equis.

Despite the feast, the day leaves me beaten, and depletion oozes out from every corner. A meager, unclear urine flow, sign of imminent dehydration, persists and is doubly unsettling.

A moonless night arrives, and I build no fire due to the scarcity of down wood. The silence is instant and absolute. I feel alien, visible, naked. On an impulse, I howl. My cry evaporates swiftly in the thin air, gobbled by stillness and the cold objectivity of the stars. Then, like a boomerang, it returns, closely followed by a second. Far down the canyon, a duo of coyotes answer my call. As a self-styled drifter, I now resemble an unsure intruder without a past.

My bed is a sand carpet under the Aqua Caliente bridge. I drift off to the sound of a soft wind sighing through the piñons. The gentle night drapes me in motionless rest, and I sleep better than any night since I started.

Am I doing this run out of boredom, for ego, to be embraced? Am I avoiding commitment, relationships? Am I performing an eternal penance? Or, could I be hoping for a permanent haven from the real world, trying to find a niche where my piece of the puzzle might fit?

Day 4 - July 13.   The fourth day has me negotiating a recently built section of the trail highlighted by skirting across the shoulder of Bucksnort Mountain. On this ponderous 30-miler, every stream is dry. Two tagged water caches left by Anza fireman and friend, Jose Torres, who hiked them in the night before, are my only liquid. Jose sidestepped several rattlers in the process. His previous tales of their abundance in the area make me more than marginally apprehensive. The mountain mercifully offers shade, making the upward trek bearable.

A low limb nearly tackles me when it catches the bow of my shoe-string. I recover to find an unexpected cache of orange, bagel, Pepsi, and a written "Godspeed" salute from T.J. Key, topnotch trail runner and founder of the Flatlanders Ultrarunning Club. He drove five hours round trip from San Diego to leave it under a manzanita bush near an unmarked trailhead. He tried to track me down earlier, but this is rough country with a myriad of intersection arteries, and we were unable to make a connection.

T. J. went from 220 pounds and three packs of cigarettes a day in 1976 to 175 pounds in 1978, while doing 50 marathons. Ultrarunners love to break bread together. They can easily afford several thousand calories daily to replenish the energy expenditure from running long distances.

Anza newspaper editor, Carl Long, now paces me the final 1,000 yards into town. I buy him a beer at Terwilliger Store. Tonight he will treat me to a hot meal, tape an informal interview, then invite me to be a guest at his church. A pre-mailed delicacy of nut-laden fruit and huge oatmeal cookies overwhelms the potent scent of sage in ghostly still air.

I find that of all my encounters with wildlife, the rattlers make me the most anxious. A runner is on top of them much faster than a hiker. The snake doesn't have as much time to slither off, which it will normally do if it realizes you are coming. My relatively unannounced approach could startle a serpent, producing a defensive reaction. Since these notoriously maligned rascals have poor eyesight and the inability to hear like humans, they utilize ground vibrations, heat, and a keen sense of smell to pinpoint impending danger.

Contrary to legend, rattlesnakes will be more numerous in the over-grown segments of Northern California than in the Mojave and Anza Borrego deserts. I will most likely encounter them at dawn or dusk when they are foraging. One soon develops a profound respect. I concentrate my cadence on the sunny side of the trail where visibility is better and hidden habitats are more easily avoided.

Rattlers have a penchant for water and tend to frequent fire scarred areas. They don't necessarily vacate the path or emit their infamous warning. If you are lucky, the one you meet will have just gorged himself with a rodent in which case it will be venomless for a few days. During their eight months of non-hibernation wanderings, rattlers search out only about a dozen meals. Being territorial, they may travel only several hundred yards in their lifetime.

Day 5 - July 14. On this first rest day, as in others to follow, I read, write, try to find a jacuzzi, have a cold beer, fill the fuel tank with hot pasta or pancakes, and recopy my trip log. I study my topo maps to prepare me for the upcoming real estate. I walk around town and make new friends. In my experience, I find that country people are better listeners, generally live longer, and usually clean their plates — all admirable traits.

I spend the night in an unused trailer at Kamp Anza Kampground, courtesy of Terry and Marilynn Grant. Early morning church services in a tiny barn offer my first reconnection with the world of seven-day weeks that I left behind, which now seems ages ago.

Already my feet are battered and callused. I sand them down and thoroughly work antifungal cream into the crusting cracks. The daily washing of feet and socks minimizes the damage somewhat.

Day 6 - July 15. At dawn I feel renewed. That in itself is a relief. I surge with vim and verve northeast towards Santa Rosa Summit, then up the arduous Desert Divide Trail to visit newly found friend (via a chance meeting in Anza), Mitch Regal, at a private ranch. A huge fire had ravaged the canyon three days earlier. Denuded gulches dot the barren forest like a charred checkerboard. The day's endeavor is predominantly uphill on soft, rich earth and goes smoothly. It is the first day of bearable temperatures with dimly veiled thunderheads providing a buffer between the sun and the earth.

The ranch is primitive and the only sign of human life for a half dozen miles. A shower, beer, and hot meal leave me feeling grateful for the creature comforts I'd like to think I will never take for granted again.

On this night, so still but for the far-off chant of coyotes, sleep pulls me in feet first. I am too tired to think. I am awakened at dawn by the bellowing screech of a distant horned owl. It seems to be laughing at its own joke — possessing some eerie sense of humor.

Vertical Trail Animal

Day 7 - July 16. At 8 a.m. I run toward Idyllwild at elevations approaching 9,000 feet. The trail is the steepest I have encountered so far — scree strewn with precipitous ledges. High on a ridge, a badly eroded washout had taken a couple of horses to their deaths a week earlier when they plunged over the side. One rider was nearly killed. He was part of a family of four doing as much of the California portion of the Pacific Crest Trail as time allowed. Their trip was over.

The grade is slightly over 15%. I feel like the trail is vertical. I have averaged close to a marathon a day for six days, most of it uphill.

At the top of Apple Canyon, I find a surprise water cache left by Anza resident and friend, Tim Lauridsen. The large label bearing my name and a neatly printed good luck message infuse me with motivation on the rocky, uphill jaunt. The glare, intensified by reflections on the granite, causes my eyes to ache. I turn them upward, toward my destination, and give in to feelings of raw anticipation as I heave myself through a maze of trail configurations.

A sleek, fleet-winged hawk swoops down from nowhere, searching for prey. Its sharp eyes constantly scan the ground below, and, in an abrupt move, the hawk slams its wings in reverse to stop in midair. It hovers a moment, then dives toward my torso, and at the last moment pulls up short, swishing past and upward again without losing speed. It perches in a treetop and squawks mercilessly as if I am invading a territorial nest or coming dangerously close to a mating area. The message is clear. I quickly leave the domain of this animated fighter plane.

For a moment, I am reminded of a good friend's encounter with a huge raven on a mountain trail near here. He was viciously attacked and left with his bald head well bloodied.

Nearing Idyllwild, I wind down Devil's Slide trail for replenishment at Hilltop Sandwich Shop (now Kathi's Pastries). After receiving me like a truly honored guest, they treat me to soup, chili, a massive hot turkey sandwich, and blueberry cobbler. I hole up in a basement under a garage for the night, and look forward to my second rest day.

Day 8 - July 17. Walking through Idyllwild this morning I almost feel like an intruder. As if by virtue of this special mission I am somewhat different than those around me. I write 20 postcards, some with fairly typical messages, but the irony of the effort strikes me. Instead of being drawn into civilization, I have the sense that these occasional stopovers in towns could upset my will and persistence. I already knew just how critical these rest days would be and that I'd have to make peace with the ritual.

The Pogo Stick Run

Day 9 - July 18. It is a privilege to entertain my first pacer since I left Mexico. Jose Torres, the fireman who'd left me the much needed water the week before, joins me on this 26-miler which culminates with a nearly 8,000-foot trail descent, the greatest west of the Rockies.

In just under 150 miles of running I have crossed only one stream — a mere trickle in Little Tahquitz Valley. "No one" runs the desert part of this trail in the summer months. Even the backpackers stay away. I won't see a hiker until well into the San Gabriel mountains, a full 19 days along my journey.

We ease up Fuller Ridge, then begin the 19-mile downward plunge through Snow Creek Canyon to the desert floor at Whitewater. It calls for precision footwork as we tightrope through a maze of manzanita and sage.

Just to the east lies an abrupt mountain face — cliffs only bighorn sheep and mountain climbers can scale — that passes through several ecological zones from palms to pines. In few places do both alpine and desert vegetation thrive in such close proximity.

At noon a sudden storm hurls huge hailstones at us, and the lightning is so close that it rattles the ground. The hail stings our cheeks, burns our backs, and then builds up beneath us, making some of the smooth rocks slippery. The graying sky is punctuated by blue flashes of terror — our adrenalin is pumping. We make a hectic sprint toward lower and friendlier territory.

Later today we will learn that 100 people were evacuated by helicopter from an adjacent plateau above the Palm Springs tramway. Ironically, among them would be one of my pacers, Kent Holder, outstanding ultra athlete and a close friend. He had experienced the secondary stages of hypothermia while on a solo 20-mile trail run in that area.

The stormy fusillade follows us for some time. Attempts to outpace it are futile. A couple of times I thought the lightning would transform us into slabs of fried bacon.

We are so wrapped up in the storm that I hardly notice the bee sting in my calf which is sore and swelling. Halfway down the hill, two well disguised rattlers cross the trail. The morning has been so intense that it is difficult to muster yet another surge of adrenalin. My heart is pounding as we detour with chilling trepidation. I steal another glance at the rattlers, marveling at how closely they match the terrain. What I cannot say is expressed by the reverberating echoes of the storm in the canyons, which ricochet like gun shots.

I might have dreaded heights, lightning, poisonous snakes, and public speaking in the past, but I got three out of four here.

It seems the wind blows through my ears and burns the backs of my eyeballs as it whistles through. Cold, oxygen depleted air irritates an already slightly sore throat. We descend with intense concentration; our mental controls locked on automatic pilot. Each breath strains my lungs to capacity. Time seems to slip away as I find an already fragile grasp on reality rapidly dissolving.

A brightly painted rainbow flickers over a knife-edge ridge, suffusing the land with an uncanny peace, as the ominous deluge finally eases off. The balance of mother nature has made me aware of my daily anxieties and impossible urges.

Jose departs, and I am mercifully whisked off for a nocturnal thaw-out in Palm Springs at the dry abode of longtime running friends, John and Kitty Emig. The aura of civilization and its tamed landscape strike a sharp contrast to the day's events.

Day 10 - July 19.   A gathering dawn mandates regaining all that lost elevation. My second pacer, Barry Hawley, close friend and founder of the San Juan Trail 50-Miler, joins me for the climb.

Today's run has us alternately struggling through soft sand and rock-hopping dozens of stream beds as we circumvent the outrageously eroded terrain up toward Heart Bar. Within minutes of departing we encounter the second largest, and by far, noisiest rattler of the trek. Dominating the trail, it barks an ominous warning. An endless barrage of soft missile tosses by Barry, affectionately known as "Baz," has little effect. He finally gets his point across with a stunning, persuasive direct hit at which point the reptile heads off to a more secluded habitat. After witnessing the double-figure parade of "misses," I determine that my well-meaning friend does not come from a background of team sports that involve throwing. Who says God doesn't have a sense of humor?

Rattlesnake barrage   by Mike Dirham

The hour that follows is punctuated by the silent canyon flight of a solitary golden eagle. This expansive glider stops us both in our tracks. For a few moments, I feel very small.

Just to our left, Southern California's highest peak, 11,499-foot Mt. San Gorgonio, punctuates the high spine of the San Bernardino mountains.

It is destined to be an action-packed day. By midmorning we are squishing up the trail trying to find shelter from a brand new deluge. Superlative ultrarunner Maurie Bosquet, having shuttled himself to our destination by car, runs down the path to join us. The rumbling thunder resembles faraway fireworks, and the lightning, though it strikes far to the northeast, stops me each time it hits. At noon the sky is a canopy of darkness, black as a moonless night.

A week ago, nearing dehydration in the desert, I prayed for the water that is causing me so much discomfort now. Twice in the last hour, conditions have approximated flash flooding with veritable liquid sheets moving down the mountain as if on wheels. After a long period of drought in some area of the country, you will often read of a flood soon afterward that causes considerable damage. It is as if nature reminds us that she is in control, and that surprise visitations of her vehemence should be expected.

The ceaseless, face-pecking rain is becoming more than a nuisance now. Even with my cap on, the rain is obstructing my vision. I know I must keep my eyes open under these conditions; I could tumble in any second. Nonetheless, I am overcome by the desire to close them to keep out the water, and go forward half blindly.

At Heart Bar the journey's end finds us greeted by tomorrow's pacer, John Emig, along with a dry shelter and a hot meal prepared by Kitty. The feeling of gratitude takes on a new meaning for me. By the time I reach Canada, I will have thrown out whatever shallowness I formerly attached to that word.

I offer Baz and Maurie a warm embrace and heartfelt thanks, then bid them adieu.

Somewhere else it is Friday night with end-of-the-work-week celebrating and a few motionless hours in front of the tube — all those "normal" activities that seem so foreign.

Big Bear Bound

Day 11 - July 20. John Emig, former Meet Director of the Palm Springs 50-Miler, rejoins me today for the wet grind northwest to Big Bear. The trail is shaded by towering Jeffrey pines, and there is a sense of being protected — a change from the treeless landscape that has prevailed until now. It resembles a long, aboveground tunnel. Several of these imposing sentinels are strikingly large in girth. Sheltering limbs, as thick as oil drums, bear testimony to their age. The air is sweet with the smell of sap.

This scenario proves to be a carbon copy of yesterday as John and I press on in makeshift rainwear — two mobile trash bags loping in harmony over Onyx Summit. The sky is as dirty as dishwater. A violent headwind hinders our efforts and lashes the beaded rainwater onto our foreheads and into our eyes. We languish like shriveled gazelles in this woodsy haven.

During this session of relentless uphill running, my calves are somewhat better, having responded favorably to my evening icing rituals. There is still residual swelling and pain from last week's bee sting. To complicate matters, my right shoe is beginning to break down due to pounding on the angled rubble. The pack weight doesn't help either. I worry that my shoes won't hold up until next Wednesday when I will get a replacement pair.

Water and fresh melon — on two stops — are today's only sustenance, provided by John's excited wife, Kitty.

This night, I make my bed on the floor of the "Team Big Bear" bike shop. A well-worn rug provides a buffer from the floor's cold, hard surface. I'm dry and warm, so to me it is like paradise.

Day 12 - July 21. I awaken to a much needed rest day which opens with a blueberry waffle and the Sunday paper. The water skiers are already on Big Bear Lake at 6 a.m. On this first cloudless day in five, I switch roles and watch the "King of the Mountain Triathlon."

Day 13 - July 22. At dawn's light on Monday, I make my way through Big Bear to the Fawnskin Cafe where I'm greeted by buckwheat hotcakes and coffee. A logger gives me a lift back to the trail, and obviously intrigued by my adventure, proffers a hearty, go-for-it handshake.

With determined vigor, I attack the corrugated topsoil that bisects this astounding wild country. Near Holcomb Creek, I meet three rattlers within an hour, sharpening my concentration. A lone bighorn pays me no mind as he ambles nonchalantly along an unstable, barren slope.

Dancing west alone, I consider that I have not seen one hiker since I left the Mexican border. My thoughts are distracted by a dust-choked throat and itchy skin that threatens to steal my focus from the trail as I tiptoe through sandy washes lined with poison oak.

This is majestic, compelling country. For comparison purposes, I make a token attempt to visualize what the traffic must be like at this moment in Los Angeles. I see a multi-colored wall of shimmering metal and hear the incessant honking emulating a discordant, distressing symphony. Serene and untrodden, the trail is magnificent. I'm glad I came.

A repeat bout with the five water bottles will enable me to collar another punishing ultra-day. I drink first from those secured on the hip pack to lighten the load, reserving the two quart-sized hand containers for the finale.

To preserve my battered feet, I insert thick felt forefoot and rubber heel pads to cushion the shock impact. At this point, the right shoe heel is completely cracked and partially torn off. I endeavor to lighten the pressure on that running shoe and pray it will last. As I do, overcompensation creates new problems when I transfer most of my body and pack weight to the other leg. That hamstring soon starts screaming on the long uphills. A short time later, the left quadricep and inner thigh both cramp, then seize up and lock altogether. I am forced to stop for mid-run stretches. Now I walk the steep downhills, pausing once to take two anti-inflammatory tablets. I seem to be running on raw nerve endings.

The halo over Big Bear is a deep azure. It beckons as the coming acreage will be hazy with wind-driven, powdery brown dust. I initially frolic, then languish in the first substantial water I've seen since the border — seven pools at Deep Creek Hot Springs. The velvet-like water flowing over the smooth rock is a welcome brace.

Following a nightcap of leftover soggy Saltines, I make my bed under a desert shrub. Well-deserved sleep is unbroken until midnight, when two German shepherds investigate my camp, smother me with affection like a long-lost friend, then amble off bewildered.

Day 14 - July 23. The sun's first rays shine on some gruesome deer remains, the possible aftermath of a mountain lion kill. A handful of brutally broken bones, mangled by a massive jaw, protrude through the inflamed flesh and bloody gashes. It is an unsettling way to start the day.

As I bound into Lake Silverwood for two double chili cheeseburgers and a swim, I meet highly credentialed ultrarunner Judy Ikenberry. She will shadow me to Cajon Junction through one of the California Pacific Crest Trail's most vandalized sections, bizarre Crowder Canyon.

Day 15 - July 24. The ensuing maze of unmarked, neglected trails makes accurate forward progress possible only by compass-aided guess-work. Judy and I loose sight of the trail and each other several times. Following our weary arrival at Cajon Junction, Judy departs and I recopy my journal at a nearby picnic table.

Tonight I stay in Crestline with resident trail runner Eric McCready who, with his sidekick Mike McMahon, will nudge me northward. I am in elite company as both are former ultra-event race champions. The late evening finds me contemplating the upcoming, certain to be sweltering, climb to Wrightwood.

Ambling Along the Angeles Crest

Day 16 - July 25. I slake down a half-gallon of liquid before today's first waffle print graces the earth. Another three quarts are barely enough for the unrelenting dry switchbacks. Up the encircling fringe of a steep one, lead pacer Mike nearly collides with a frisky bobcat as it leaps wide-eyed off into the shambled brush.

Daily interaction with the wild animals of the forest conjures up conflicting imagery as I contemplate the "civilized," high-tech trappings of density and concrete. Many of us distance ourselves so greatly from nature that we may never experience the privilege of its chance encounters. Mindless concentration on consumerism makes us lose a segment of our soul. It is good to be reminded occasionally that we are a part of something greater than ourselves.

The sight of Wrightwood, considered by many trail hikers to be the friendliest stopover en route to Canada, brings a slow grin and visions of rest. The rustic cabins at Camp Mariastella, where I spend the evening, get my seal of approval.

Day 17 - July 26. I have come to view these stationary days as critical. They keep my legs functioning, and are vital in refurbishing the thought processes. Though they involve extra miles in leaving the main trail, they are well worth it. Putting a traveler's check inside each pre-mailed cache has worked out beautifully. It seems like months, not a mere two weeks, since I left. Safety, simplicity, self-sufficiency, and fluids are the prevailing considerations, and continue to emerge as ongoing challenges.

The camp caretakers, Don and Robin Crowell, are our gracious hosts. Don (at this writing) is also Wrightwood's Mayor. I give a short talk on my wilderness adventure and step into a fresh pair of shoes. Four outstanding long-distance stalwarts — Ken Hamada, Ernie Baker, Del Beaudoin, and Ted Hill — motor in to pace me through the rugged San Gabriel Range. I met them all at various races over past years. They will fuel me for several days with pancakes, Spam, watermelon, and fellowship.

Ken is visibly amazed that I am not all beaten up, cut and scarred. I consider the source of his wonder, and find myself thanking God for exempting me from the adversity he envisioned.

I think about the two Pacific Crest Trail hikers who attempted to be the first to traverse the trail in its entirety in winter. They slipped on a blue-ice chute, high above Wrightwood, and fell to their deaths. The search-and-rescue workers later determined from their journals that they were in trouble for some time. The writing was almost illegible due to obvious hypothermic conditions.

Day 18 - July 27. A deafening send-off by 170 young Catholic girls residing at the camp lubricates my willing tear ducts. For a few moments, we all feel like Olympic-calibre athletes. I find myself flashing back to my early days of running, experiencing that incredible charge you get when a crowd demands you do your best. Duly fired up, we ascend Acorn Canyon and turn westward onto the main trail artery. Several jubilant campers tailgate us a short way in spirited animation.

The Pacific Crest Trail crosses the Angeles Crest Highway many times, creating a number of opportunities for access to support and fluids.

During simmering afternoon heat, we nap on top of 9,399-foot Mt. Baden Powell. It is a pleasant respite during today's rugged 28-miler. Honeycomb-like pinnacles blend with the cotton candy clouds for contrasting shades of light. The stillness continues to astound me. I can actually hear the air's slight movements even in the absence of rustling leaves. My hearing is becoming incredibly acute — as if it's evolving. I wonder if this really can happen — that one can actually enhance the senses through a special experience if you don't have a pre-existing disability.

Ken prepares a Spam and beans replenishing feast at tonight's secluded off-road hideaway.

Vocal sendoff at Wrightwood Catholic Girls Camp   by Ken Hamada

Day 19 - July 28. Today is my first contact with a hiker since the border. It's quite a shock. Rounding a ridge on Mt. Williamson, we practically collide with 50 Sierra Club enthusiasts. The general response, when I tell them what I am doing, is stunned disbelief. Later we run into three couples who embrace us and the concept of our journey. It is clear they have a picture of why I have accepted this challenge. That makes the encounter even more special. Despite the fact that I get my share of these motivational treasures, it is always a surprise when they occur unexpectedly.

The pencil-thin ribbon of dirt that is our byway today overlooks blissful vistas. The sky is so clear that we can see beyond the vast Los Angeles basin to the ocean, with Santa Catalina Island in the distance some 45 miles away. While running, we literally split the seam of a long conifer apron. The stillness is so absolute that it is fine-tuning my perceptions to their limit. My eyes now pinpoint the tiniest details and my ears pick up faraway hushed mountain melodies. I find this Ralph Waldo Emerson quote appropriate:

> *At the gates of the forest the man of the world is forced to leave his city estimate of great and small, wise and foolish.*

We have lunch with Will Shaw, an environmentally outspoken ranger, who is willing to help promote trail runs for small groups. He suggests we act as personal caretakers. The only discarded evidence of our passage should be the footprints we leave behind. The Forest Service normally frowns on timed runs in wilderness areas — even if well policed.

Ken Hamada would do the grunt work behind organizing a successful race in this area, partly in honor of ultrarunner Herman Kuhn. Herman knew these trails as well as anyone, and ran them almost daily. A fall down a blue-ice chute in severe weather took his life. Though I am extremely saddened by his death, I believe he would have chosen to die doing what he loved best.

Our path etches the perimeter of a natural amphitheater. After multiple stops for internal lubrication, I decide Messenger Flats is as good a camp as I will find and prepare to burrow in for the night. I bid adieu to my impeccably loyal friends whose selfless camaraderie keep body and soul intact. As they depart for more civilized environs, I quietly thank them.

Three days ago when we met, those same pacers stared at me as if I were a ghost. They clearly expected to find me much wearier than I was. However, they don't know about the spiritual injections I have received and why I really can and will make it to that other border, still some 2,300 miles away.

I build a small fire and crawl into my bivy sack. I am wearing everything I have to battle a wind-driven nocturnal frigidity. Snuggling up to the hot coals, I nod off on a full stomach as a bluejay's song suffuses the silence.

Unfriendly Trail

Day 20 - July 29. On what will be one of the toughest running days, I breakfast early on granola and dried apples, and begin the downward trek through Arrastre Canyon to the enchanting town of Acton. The laid-back town square is orderly and sports a historical theme. I tour the town in my scanty attire, gulping two separate light bites at a rustic country store. I nap under an outlying grove of trees.

The afternoon stretch that skirts Vasquez Rocks, passes north of the tiny town of Agua Dulce, and is a geometrical nightmare because of poor trail markings. An icy dip at a pastoral creekside in Bouquet Canyon is just what the trail doctor would have ordered had he been around. I follow with the ritualized massaging of lotion on the cracked skin housing the bottoms of my feet, then wash the few items of clothing I have.

A nagging case of conjunctivitis, compounded by dust particles and incessant salty sweat, is painful. Prescription eye drops provide only minimal relief.

I usually go to sleep just as darkness hits and rise at first light. I keep a journal to record not only my journey but my dreams, which grow more vivid as I dare to brush with the universal, and the accompanying perceptions that empower me to leave my heart. The stillness of the nocturnal shadows sharpens my senses and washes over my incredible fatigue.

Day 21 - July 30.   At dawn I begin a scramble through San Francis-quito Canyon to distant Lake Hughes.

The trail is the worst since the border. It is badly mangled from erosion and runs over erratic soft sand. For nearly 15 miles, the outside edge is deteriorated. When a crumbled section breaks away, the contoured chute pulls me feet first. For one seven-mile stretch, the manzanita and sharp buckthorn are periodically intertwined. Where a tiny passage is available, the briars lash out at and cut up my quads, calves, and forearms. Eventu-ally, even my knuckles are gashed by the attacking needle-sharp spines. My legs lurch during lapses in equilibrium and heave in pangs. My ankles ache from eons of overtime miles.

Gravity draws me briskly into camp. Mother Nature has drawn a lot of runner blood in this confrontation and nightfall brings stabbing edema. I truly regret not having scheduled tomorrow as a rest day. I ache at the thought of traversing similar terrain in the morning.

Tending my wounds fuels my anger about the condition of the trail. In an ideal scenario, every hiker would be required to adopt at least one mile of trail in a lifetime. It is hard work, but I can't think of a better way to glean a true appreciation for what's involved in building and maintaining one. I will later help build the new, privately funded Tahoe Rim trail.

Day 22 - July 31.   Today I reach Lake Hughes on what will be a day of power hiking interspersed with light, downhill running. The pain of yesterday's whipping and the conjunctivitis make it difficult to rise above the aggravation of dealing with another rotten trail segment. I do some mental calculations. It might take a ten-person crew just over a week to clear that horrendous seven-mile section that nearly felled me yesterday.

I think only of the upcoming rest days in Lancaster and seeing my good buddy Fred Hermann. These emotional thoughts — insignificant in another setting — alone get me through a truly tough day. My experience has borne out that such emotional lows are often followed by highs. I realize what I am counting on now — that this low period will be followed by a high period, as time moves me on. All I can do is prepare myself to let this happen, and ensure that my soul is receptive when it does.

Day 23 - August 1.   To get from Lake Hughes to Lancaster, I run on desert roads. This part of the Pacific Crest Trail has not yet been completed as of my passage.

The Dreaded Mojave

Days 24-25 - August 2-3.   I eventually wind up in front of "Hermann's Haven" (home of aforementioned Fred). I spend ten heavenly minutes walking barefoot on the soft, green grass — the first I have seen in almost a month. My toes tingle with appreciation.

I then walk to the nearest supermarket and politely borrow a beach chair that is out front for sale. I position myself comfortably in it (a short distance from shopper foot traffic) and devour the Sunday paper, along with several ice cold libations. I'm "livin!"

Fred and ultrarunner Rich Dinges will team up to pace me over the vast, scorched carpet known as the Mojave Desert. Fred's lovely wife, Velma, prepares gourmet pasta and their special "Hermann Bread." Velma Hermann's bread (it's a sweet bread with an Italian theme) is famous not only for its unbelievably delicious flavor, but for the painstaking preparation it involves. Fred says it takes 14 days from the time the dough ingredients are assembled to its grand arrival from the oven, and that its delicious aroma fills the air for days afterward.

Pacers follow Author through San Gabriel Mountains   by Del Beaudoin

In mustering assistance for this trek, I am surprised at how willingly it was offered. My friends feel that they are somewhat obligated to me for my coaching of them in the past.

This was true with Fred, a 25-year officer of the California Highway Patrol who sees his share of stress. It had begun to take its toll on him and he was looking for a way to turn his life around when I met him ten years ago. Fred likes to talk about how our relationship developed and often reminisces about the many adventures and misadventures we've had. He's been such a pivotal figure in my life and it only seems appropriate to have him share his thoughts on this journey:

> "I am here with Bob on this historic journey because I owe him in a big way. Without running, I don't know what my life would be like now. And his help in the early years — when I honestly believed I couldn't take another 50 yards on the trail — kept me going.
>
> Bob's 'trail etiquette' is unmatched. Basically, he will do whatever you ask, if it means it will help you reach a personal milestone. You can't believe how flattered I was by his unflagging assistance. All he ever asked was that I make a 'strong, honest effort' — he'd do the rest.
>
> One thing he does insist on in return, though, is that I always bring him some of Velma's bread. Once when he was working registration at the Wild, Wild West Marathon in Lone Pine, California, he greeted me with the words: 'you can't sign up until you give me a piece of Hermann Bread.' Luckily, I had some with me.
>
> I would venture that two out of three long distance runners know Bob; after all, he's been on trails all over the country, and run in more races than I can count. Many of us think of him as the guru of off-road running — although he's not what you'd call a 'pretty' runner (you can't really see his talent in his style, and he is far from graceful).
>
> Somehow, though, he's always been different from the rest of us, and most ultra athletes I know will enter a competition in part to be near Bob and the tremendous positivity he radiates. He sings these funny little songs on the trails and has his own code of ethics which stipulates that 'when you get to the top of the hill, you always wait for the rest of the pack' and 'you never pop a beer until the last person's in.' He taught me how to estimate the

time by strategic placement of measured hand-widths between the sun and the horizon — I sometimes find myself doing this unconsciously, even when I'm far from a trail.

He has his quirks, that's for sure. He refuses to run on concrete and brings his dog whenever he can. I had to laugh Super Bowl Sunday when he brought his beagle 'Blazer' in a Baby Jogger and ran the entire race with the puppy riding in front of him.

I'd follow the guy anywhere; I attribute most of the positive changes in my life to him."

For more than an hour I savor the peace of being in a special place with good friends. I work gobs of Aloe Vera lotion into my leathery skin, in preparation for the upcoming Mojave crossing. The anxiety I felt in preparing for this section creeps up from within. My heart flutters and I try to calm a racing brain that flashes visions of the Mojave Green.

The Mojave Green is California's most feared rattler, having a greater venom potency than any other reptile in the western United States. Swelling and gangrene can set in so quickly, that unless a bite is treated within several hours, the only options may be amputation or possible death. The smaller snakes, who haven't yet learned to conserve venom, can be the most dangerous. We will traverse their arid pathways in the early morning hours in an attempt to stay ahead of the heat. This is the time when the Mojave Green tends to roam most freely.

As I drift off into sleep, my hands clasp together, I find myself praying without having planned to.

Day 26 - August 4   At 5:30 a.m. in Lancaster, California, bathed in the incandescent glow of a cracker-jack sunrise, I set out with adrenalin pumping and spirits in high gear. The unseasonably cool 95-degree weather is appreciated. Half-eaten jack rabbit carcasses abound. The heat radiating from the ground causes us to take in voluminous amounts of fluid. Fred acts as desert safari guide since he seems to know every step of the terrain personally.

But enough about Fred. Rich Dinges, the third member of our trio today, deserves special mention. In the running world, Rich Dinges is looked upon as little short of a miracle man. When he suffered a serious bicycle accident some years ago, his prospects for recovery were called slim. The orthopedists said he would never walk again.

Clearly, Rich not only didn't believe them but began that bleak day determined to turn this prognosis around. Enduring considerable pain, Rich designed his own course of therapy. Within two years he was walking again. Today he is an accomplished, recovering ultrarunner. The only evidence of that frightful event that threatened to rob him of physical freedom is a slight hampering limp. I always feel honored when he is around. His strength sets riveting standards for the rest of us.

We follow the barren road shoulder as screeching sand flurries pepper my nearly numb eyeballs. I pull down the visor a notch and adjust my bandanna so that the widest part covers the back of my neck. There is cinder dust in every orifice. Salt-caked sweat irritates my parched lips.

The Mojave, though monotonous, is spiritually nourishing with its sounds and smells. The coyote kingdom provides a symphony of eerie howling, baying, and yipping. One lonely soul blasts the still air with an anthem of praise that must have made the rest of its friends jealous.

My senses are confused. Our nostrils try to sift the scents as we come across them — the animal fur, scat, and vomit — but these must compete with the stench of sweat. Between the footfalls on the crusty terrain, I can pick out the sound of my heart beating. Its regular thumping provides solace during these miles of sameness and simplicity.

I wear a sun hat with flaps and a long-sleeve white shirt, saturating both regularly with water. I consume such voluminous amounts of fluid that I often urinate to the side while moving. I have so much practice, I can clear both skin and cloth with unerring effectiveness.

After passing a few hikers along the way with crusted mouth sores, I work to avoid both lip and crotch-chafing problems before they become severe. The frequent use of Labiosan, Micatin, and hydrocortisone cream helps immeasurably.

Author is paced through southern part of Mojave Desert   by Danny Kessler

The consistent use of sunscreen is a must, as well as an enormous coddling of the legs with lotion. I use an ultraviolet block with a 15+ potency. One place I do not put it is on my cap-protected forehead where dripping sweat might cause it to filter down into my eyes.

Earlier, a horrendous siege of knotty jungle rot surfaced on both heels. The skin hardened and cracked because of the loss of moisture and elasticity. My daily foot-saving ritual highlights powder and antifungal cream. I change socks frequently.

Successes over serious physical discomforts take place through planning and support, not luck. So many times I said a "Hail Mary" for the supplies that John Pagliano and Bruce Letvin prepared for me. Real satisfaction stems when all goes smooth, distinguishing adventure from stunt.

Today's sandstorm finally subsides. Fred, Rich, and I are squired back from near the town of Mojave to the Hermanns' suburban ranch to steam clean our body hair and skin pores. I reflect with trepidation on the waterless, poorly-signed stretches that lie ahead.

Day 27 - August 5. I am returned to a road shoulder just beyond the town of Mojave. As I grasp for the courage and strength to skirt barren Jawbone Canyon, running guardian angel John Anderson steps in. He will pace me on a stark, nightmarish segment, blitzed by dirt bikes and dune buggies. A demolition derby of unpoliced maniacs have desecrated the wilderness with their spinning tire tread. It takes some persistent thought to rid myself of the anger I'm feeling.

We seem surrounded by indefatigable creosote that survive by raw tenacity in this thorny place. Billowing cloud puffs dance like loose cotton against a backdrop of juniper foothills that form a gateway to the lower Sierra. A snoozing rattler, three feet long and half a dozen buttons proud, is digesting a recent meal by burping a bulge down his body length. Awakened by our approach, it stares, darts its tongue, and slides off quickly.

We are severely taxed by the stretch through Butterbredt Canyon which bears little resemblance to the map so diligently studied. A neat guy and mountain runner from Ridgecrest, John is about my age and skinny as a rail. We make quite a pair — two moving sticks punctuating the shapes and shades of a changing horizon.

The terra cotta buttes are too rugged to run across. We are relegated to finding the unsigned passable route through them, intently concentrating on where we put our feet. We appear to be unwelcome guests in this arid, difficult wilderness.

Cutting across shredded gullies to a sandy wash, we weave uphill by some dry springs to a well. The windmill is not pumping water. The sheer fragility of this outdoor carpet — its appearance of having rarely been crossed — bespeaks caution. Dodging the saguaro and cholla cacti that resemble outpost lookouts, we drink every drop of water from the extra bottles we carry. John's loyal family greets us, a bedraggled duo, with fluids at Kelso Valley Road. Tonight's nocturnal respite is at the Anderson home.

Day 28 - August 6.   A 30-mile, ten-hour day follows a dreamless sleep. John's wife, Janet, will again rescue our parched throats at improvised aid stations. The run by Skinner Peak to Walker Pass is steaming hot and relentless with its monumental climbs.

We stop for a trail snack within the protective lee of a large sunlit boulder. It takes seemingly endless footstrikes to reach our afternoon destination. We ramble down the bone-jarring trail; our quads and calves burning from lactic acid buildup. John and I let out a whoop of wild exhilaration as we sight the pass. That first cold libation is incomprehensibly awesome — nectar from a higher source. We ice the quads and place leftover cubes inside our white caps.

I find hard effort, calculated risk, and stirring adventure to be basic human needs. They are the spiritual vitamins of life.

John and Janet again house me, then John shuttles me back in the morning to where I head solo into the Kern watershed.

Ecology Zone Survey

Day 29 - August 7.   Because I look quite vulnerable as a gangly, shirtless runner, my animal intensity softens. I feel the sublime rebirth of a pioneer. I am treated to the spectacle of a dozen frolicking deer who seem to accept me graciously into their arena.

Around midafternoon I stop for a dip in a lucent pool on the South Fork of the Kern River. For a full 30 minutes, I cavort like a kid at a favorite swimming hole, bobbing and clambering in and out of the water, having abandoned my meager apparel on the bank.

In that rare state of mixed relief and utter fatigue, I lie comatose on bladed granite, gratefully soaking up the sun's cleansing rays.

Lumbering, fat cattle are plentiful at streamside, so I avoid filling my bottles. Cattle can contaminate water. Not long ago, a Pacific Crest Trail hiker picked up a serious case of bacterial meningitis after drinking at a contaminated hot spring.

Simple granola chunks are a daily diet staple. I continue to consume it although it is unbearably bland. Salted crackers help keep my sodium level up.

Today I encounter a hiker living on kibbled dog food. He assures me that it has the highest nutritional components and contains all eight amino acids.

As I amble into Kennedy Meadows, one of my worst fears becomes a reality. A pre-mailed survival cache isn't there. It will not show up for nine months when it is finally discovered by hiker Rena Gallant as she passes through. Despite gnawing uncertainty about how I will fend in the stretch ahead without trail food, I wolf down an extra large dinner at an outside cafe and sleep blissfully in a barnyard.

Day 30 - August 8. Midway through the following rest day, I am sitting on a flat stump having a cold brew. Hometown compatriots Brian McBean and Bruce Johnson drive up separately. Brian is a solid journeyman trail runner, and Bruce is a former high school distance champion. I am overwhelmed by their generosity as this visit is unexpected. Hearing tales of my ongoing endeavor gave them a vicarious itch, so they decide to track me down and share the spirit.

Tonight, the pacer I do expect, outstanding ultramarathoner Hal Winton, spins into the campground. We are now a safari foursome for the next two days. Hal has been an age-class record holder at Colorado's grueling Pikes Peak Marathon. He is also Race Day Director of the Angeles Crest 100-Miler.

My outdoor bedroom cushion is two six-inch-square ensolite pads tucked under the shoulder and hip. While running I place them between the fanny pack and my hipbones. This keeps the punishing bulk from bashing my tender membranes.

Day 31-32 - August 9-10. We head out at a decent pace across a landscape that appears recently incinerated. At a sandstrip bordering a rivulet we are treated to diverse vistas of glorious meadows. A symphony of melodious frog songs, emitted by thimble-sized voice boxes, soothe our spirits.

To the east are a myriad of impassable canyons that lead to the high desert of Owens Valley. Just ahead is a box canyon that balances a truce line between tundra and forest. Tall, majestic pines hunch their shoulders, filtering colors that splash seductive tints upon the springy brown-needle surface.

The trail takes a wandering horseshoe pattern and spans a verdant valley. I feel cloistered in this enchanted place where stillness abounds. The surrounding woods are spanking clean and simple in their magnificence. It was Byron who may have best put it into words:

> *To sit on rocks, to muse o'er flood and fell,*
> *To slowly trace the forest's shady scene,*
> *Where things that own not man's dominion dwell,*
> *And mortal foot hath ne'er or rarely been;*
> *To climb the trackless mountain all unseen, . . .*
> *This is not solitude, 't is but to hold*
> *Converse with Nature's charms and view her stores unroll'd.*

In a trance-like state, we hammer down Mulkey Pass into Cottonwood Basin. We encounter an excited John Middleton, accomplished mountain climber and triathlete, who drives us into Lone Pine for some hard-earned rest and relaxation. I embrace my support foursome and wish them a safe drive.

Days 33-34 - August 11-12. I spend two days with Robert and Gayle Frickel, two of Owens Valley's more rugged and finer citizens. Robert is a co-creator of the Wild, Wild West Marathon, an annual trail race through arid cacti and the lore-laden Alabama Hills of California. I stay in a small shed next to their mountain home which has no telephone or electricity. The water supply comes through a quarter-mile-long hose leading from an underground spring.

We utilize three hours picking fresh fruit in a protected reserve, giving most of it away to local seniors and residents of an outlying Indian reservation.

The Frickel's epitomize the wholesome country life. They are usually more congenial than city folks and live a less stressful, laid-back lifestyle. They seem more enthusiastic, are extremely unselfish, and often have greater longevity.

This is a welcome rest stop before tackling the Sierra. I have run this next stint several times in the past. California's lower elevation segment is pretty much behind me: To the peaks!

South of Mulkey Pass near Olancha Peak   by Hal Winton

3 The Soaring Sierra _____

Climb the mountains and get their good tidings. Nature's peace will flow into you as sunshine flows into trees. The winds will blow their own freshness into you, and the storms their energy, while cares will drop off like autumn leaves.

— John Muir
My First Summer in the Sierra

Friends and Fun

Day 35 - August 13. With a mixed sense of adventure and foreboding, I step out to make my way into "bear country." My companion today is "Buffalo Bill" McDermott, perennial Catalina Island marathon champion. He is also one of the nation's top ultradistance trail runners. Though it is his first run at this altitude, he coaxes me through the Mt. Whitney area for two arduous 25-mile days. Close to ninety percent of the terrain is above 10,000 feet. Bill revels at being able to drink in exquisite timberline vistas that fortify us both as we climb over the raw-boned topography.

This is something Bill has never been able to experience due to the tremendous concentration required by high-speed trail racing. An engineer by training, Bill can't resist the urge to periodically readjust my fanny pack for optimum position and snugness to keep it from thrashing around.

We stride on. Exhilarated, our limbs move almost of themselves in harmony with the high country. A cloudless sky, punctuated by the radiant sun, offers a glorious greeting. This alone blots out the low points of the excursion's unthinkable soreness and fatigue. Stately citadels soar above us. Narrow-throated gullies below resemble yawning chasms. A rock falling nearby echoes through the crisp air causing a trembling in my muscles before they regain command. I feel the presence of a guardian angel as I visualize a protective aura.

Buzzing flies drone, jays chatter, and the chipmunks hurry and stir incessantly. The latter proudly guard this alpine gateway with thickly furred breasts pushed out, ears alertly poised, and heads arched smartly upward and back. These roving mountain dwellers sing melodiously, trumpeting through the forest spires.

We suck in deep breaths, trying to barter for an acceptable exchange of our carbon dioxide for the scarce oxygen at this altitude. Bad weather or altitude sickness defeat half the hikers in this area. The symptoms of altitude sickness begin with severe headache, usually progress to nausea,

Toting fanny pack along Sierra trail   by Robert Frickel

and finally inertia. If afflicted, it is imperative to drink plenty of fluids and get to a lower elevation.

This primitive form of running, that propels one through open space on timberline routes, allows me to view life from a new perspective. How many people ever get to see anything comparable to this? How truly lucky I feel to celebrate this affirmation: I experience a perfect place at a perfect time without owning it. I use my lowest gears to make the ascents, and the effort puts me at my highest element. I feel like a modified Henry Thoreau on the move.

In the wild, the human is valued as an individual. Back in the "real world" (what a weird connotation that is, for what is the "real world" after all?), we are often treated as a mere member of the masses, shunted about in a mechanized society. This experience reawakens my true individual spirit and gives me a forever altered sense of purpose. All around me are glossy domes in the alpenglow and I comprehend a new understanding of the purposes of God. I tuck these visions into a treasured place as we approach tonight's camp and a waiting friend.

Dario Malengo, wilderness ranger at Crabtree Meadow, provides us with a meal of hot lasagna in this high-perched paradise. Conversation focuses on the earsplitting noise of the jets that earlier in the day buzzed the top of Mt. Whitney. Whether out of sport or boredom, the pilots terrified a good number of hikers with their dangerous actions.

Other campfire topics include bears and giardia. The latter is caused by a water-borne bacterial cyst transmitted in the feces of humans and over 40 species of animals.

Exhausted from the day's exertion, we drop onto rusty bunk beds in Dario's tiny wilderness cabin and avoid confronting the opportunistic black bears that prowl the area. The scent of food accidentally spilled onto one's gear would likely attract their ravenous appetites. Dario recounts stories of several backpackers who lost all their supplies due to inadequate "bear bagging." It is recommended that wilderness travelers hang their food from the Park Service cables suspended between smooth cylindrical poles that cannot be climbed by animals. Another option is to transfer all food, toothpaste, and any other aromatic substance into a stuff bag, and cinch it securely at the end of ten yards of sturdy rope. You toss it over a large overhead limb, high enough to keep the dangling goodies above the reach of an upright bear, and counter-balance the free end with a rock.

We learn of one ingenious sow who hoists one of her cubs piggyback on her shoulders. This well-coached protège then rises to a standing position and swats the food sack like a piñata, dumping its contents and providing the entire family with a nocturnal feast.

If you are awakened by such a commotion, you don't want to risk injury by attempting to retrieve your possessions. You invite a charge by getting between mama and her cubs. Once the bear has your stuff, it is hers. If she gets all your gear, your trip may be over, but at least you are intact.

By contrast, marmots are relentless daytime bandits and can strip you clean while you are swimming or climbing a nearby peak. Like smaller bears, they appear cuddly but can be ferocious when agitated.

I am reminded of a comical after-dark intrusion on Catalina Island by an unpredictable wild pig. It ripped open my daypack, left all the food, but ate the soap and toothpaste.

Day 36 - August 14. After a breakfast of steaming oatmeal, honey biscuits, and hot tea, Bill and I run for two hours with Dario through his jurisdiction. We help him pick up litter on this bone-chilling morning, then head off on the remainder of a grueling 26-miler that propels us to Vidette Meadow's streamside oasis.

The wind blasts us on the ridges and screeches overhead as we zigzag through forested U-shaped hollows. Neon-winged grasshoppers crackle in tempo. A rhapsody of critter music echoes from the lakelets and ponds. A tiny frog leaps from the grass over my feet as his lonely companion croaks huskily in the background.

Bill hyperventilates while skinny dipping in an 11,000-foot alpine lake on Bighorn Plateau. The run at altitude has taxed his oxygen intake, and he struggles to regain a comfortable equilibrium. He is aware that this is a small price to pay for the upcoming privilege of viewing the panorama at 13,180-foot Forester Pass on this impeccably clear day.

Soon afterward, we stand together in respectful awe astride that pass, the highest pass on the Pacific Crest Trail.

During a 1,000-foot, switchback-riddled drop north of the pass, three mule deer bound from the trail and scramble through battered vegetation. The leader's glare indicates a belligerence that human intruders would dare interfere with his running free in this wild sanctuary.

Ten miles further on, Bill and I provoke curious glances and gasping queries from hikers as we wind along delicate grass tendrils toward Vidette Meadow's velvet rug.

At twilight, though the sun has barely left the sky, temperatures are in the high 40's. Our dramatic shirtless arrival amongst the other campers, wearing only shorts, fanny packs and visors, brings back memories of winning a regional cross-country championship as a spunky youth.

After nestling in by a group fire, we meet Lew and Joanna Knickerbocker, a friendly couple from the Mt. Lassen area. They have recently married and are spending 40 days hiking the trail. At dawn, they casually commented: "We would like to assist you next summer when you pass through Lassen National Park. You will experience some real hospitality."

A year later when I eventually accept, the Knickerbockers will treat me to a trailside "Carbo-Feast," trailhead shuttles, and two nights of pure creature comfort. Strangers are just friends you haven't met yet. I believe you lose if you don't make the effort to find them.

A great stretch of trail   by Bob Carpenter

I lay my bed in the notch of a piney thicket under a canopy of webbed
limbs. My camp is wind-protected by a bladed rock and a large fallen log.
A thick pine-needle carpet makes it as snug as a squirrel's nest. Despite

the cold, it is one of the best nocturnal mountain chambers I would find anywhere on the Pacific Crest Trail.

Gardens of Eden

Day 37 - August 15. This morning I concentrate on the delicate chirping of the birds during a bright sunrise. Nearby tantalizing scents cleanse my pipes. The calm stillness implies a lasting tranquility. I luxuriate in this alpine paradise. Happiness is not a station you arrive at but a manner of traveling.

Bill and I inch noiselessly up steep, rocky footing. We are soon rewarded with more playful deer-family frolicking. We sight a happy Bob Carpenter, Southern California running buddy, at a signed junction near Charlotte Lake. Bob has just driven solo for five hours on his motorcycle with a care package. He hiked it in over Kearsarge Pass, along with a six-pack of ice cold beer in an insulated bag. It's only 10 a.m., but it matters little in this scenario. We celebrate right on the trail with a high-energy meal.

Bill runs back with Bob to rejoin civilization, and I am left to whisper to the gods. Alone, I run upward toward the remote, lake-studded cirque below Glen Pass. Jays and juncos chirp with heart-intoxicating sweetness just above the timberline fringe of the dense forest.

I catch up with Val Fulsebakke, whom I have never met, hiking solo. She had been out several days with a couple of hiking friends, but they lacked proper conditioning for the many climbs at altitude and eventually were forced to leave the trail. She is determined to finish her planned trek on her own — she will.

We do some nimble boulder scrambling over rough terrain to Glen Pass. We descend separately along a shark-finned ridgeline among a smattering of lakelets that highlight our passage into a living amphitheatre of grandeur. Eloquent monuments watch over the glacial recesses as we meet for a lunch date at Rae Lakes.

A pond in the basin beckons. Val and I decide to take a dip. We both screech when we bubble up from our frigid immersion, our cries shattering the stillness. It feels like an ultimate transgression to pierce the silence so. Fearing possible frostbite of intimate body parts, we get out after five minutes. After sharing snacks, we bask in the sun's warmth — lying on the feathery tapestry of this sub-alpine paradise.

Val is a veritable walking book on this area. Her thorough knowledge of wildflowers, edible plants, and berries stems from her background in botany. As we move north, Val walks as I run ahead. I wait for her at several spontaneous rest stops.

After a dangerous, late-afternoon log crossing (due to high water splashing furiously on slippery moss), we regroup and camp on the north side of Woods Creek. It has a big reputation for bears. Val and I string a

Skinny dipping in a meadow pond   by Mike Dirham

food sack over a thick, high branch and have no problems. A warm fire and rest soothe our throbbing calves. The brilliant star show above is difficult to leave, but my eyelids have begun to ache.

Day 38 - August 16. After breakfast I bid my new-found comrade, Val, adieu and strike out toward Pinchot Pass, one of the Sierra's more rugged challenges.

Water, like a companion, gains value by scarcity and isolation. I make sure I have plenty with me and within me for the vast mileage ahead. Most animals can exist for several days on the fluid they've stored in their tissues. This animal has to continually replace liquids lost through profuse sweating.

A major concern is finding safe drinking water to dissuade dehydration, cramping, and muscle fatigue. I try to drink upstream, where the water is moving vertically. I treat all streams, lakes, and ponds with iodine tablets. A filter is too bulky to carry and tends to clog with use. If I have to drink from a murky pool, I look for green vegetation and live insects that indicate marginal purity.

Iodine will eradicate most microorganism strains. I carry flagyl capsules in case I ingest one of the invisible giardia cysts which attaches itself to the wall of the small intestine. Giardia can become dormant in humans, much like syphilis, and recur periodically regardless of treatment. If afflicted, the consequences are not much fun. I also carry Lomotil for common diarrhea, which can appreciably weaken you.

One source of giardia cysts is the gamey residue of the muskrat, squirrel, and chipmunk. These unimposing creatures are everywhere. You can drink above heavily used campsites, cattle grazing areas, and horse crossings, but it is nearly impossible to get upstream of the small animals. Even the most innocent-appearing rivulet right out of a snow bank may contain cysts that can survive for months. A tantalizing gurgle from a cliffside seep might be contaminated from above.

You can't stop to boil water every time you need to drink. Some watering holes are of more questionable quality than others. When the only available water looks atrocious, you pray your "killer" iodine tabs will get rid of the bad guys.

One time I had been looking forward for 15 miles to filling my bottles at a placid oasis. When I limped in, an obese cow was basking in the pond. Often, I had to deviate my route to find marshy swamps or minuscule springs. Another day, one mossy seep and a couple of murky puddles provided the sole liquid on a ten-hour, 25-miler.

I drink a minimum of one quart of water nightly before retiring and the same amount on rising, so that I can stay ahead fluid-wise. My primary goal is to keep my urine "ironclad" clear around the clock — never discolored due to a negative balance which might invite dehydration. If you get in arrears on liquid, you're finished that day — maybe the next.

Although I endured yesterday's scary log crossing without incident, the fear that surfaced reminds me just how vulnerable I am on this journey. If I break a leg and am not spotted by hikers, it might be days until someone knows I am missing. Even then, my next support person would have to look for me across a somewhat lengthy section of the Pacific Crest Trail, not knowing where I've encountered trouble. I shudder at the thought of being injured and alone, and vow to proceed with a caution that ensures survival. For example, I vow to be especially careful on sheer, narrow ridgelines.

Besides terminating the run, a serious incident will be a disheartening blow to the many who are instrumental in getting me here. I am committing a considerable chunk of highly physical energy to this single odyssey. I am determined not to suffer a catastrophe of irreversible magnitude.

Under clear skies, the wind dishes out a crisp chill as I now grunt northward past weather-gnarled pines, algae-dappled lakelets, and clusters of mountain heather. I gaze anew at the splendor of the day.

After so much company this past week, I now run and eat solo. It feels so solitary. This is precisely when fears of taking a header, becoming hypothermic, being struck by lightning, mauled by a bear, drowning, or some other fast-happening quirk of poor judgment or bad luck creep into my emotional wiring. To counteract my loneliness, I will later get to know total strangers in every tiny re-supply depot between here and Canada. But now, I am torn by the effects of my lonely personal struggle. Sometimes, unexpected, debilitating incidents whisper so loudly in my ear that I cannot concentrate on the wildlife sounds. Often, everything hurts.

At other times, perhaps after a brisk lake swim, an exciting encounter with a hiker, or a snooze in a sunlit meadow followed by a couple of PowerBars, new life surges into my legs. Fresh strength fills my body from my toes to the top of my head, and all the pain vanishes. My heart pounds, and the tears well in my eyes, as I fly across the terrain with new-found resolve.

It's odd how a life that has gotten too comfortable can make you subconsciously long for a certain amount of misery. You develop a greater appreciation for the hard-earned gains. It is during these solitary times that I crave those moments, as I do now while struggling over Pinchot Pass. Bristling pinnacles and expansive outdoor cathedrals dominate the horizon. Occasional thunderclouds flank this stark granite world.

Traversing these timberline savannahs has meshed my body and soul into a closer harmony with the earth that produced them and offers the highest thrill a runner can experience. At this moment I feel the God-given connection between enjoying something and being able to do it well — a simple concept, but one that drives many of us to achieve a self-defined vision of individuality, and perhaps marginal greatness.

Still lost in this reverie, I wind down a long box canyon to another log crossing — this one bridging the Kings River — where I make camp tonight. My too-audible munching of trail mix is broken by the whoosh of padded hooves, as four deer let me know I have trespassed. I coax some wet twigs into flame and a small fire flickers under drooping boughs. My

Sally Keyes Lakes   by Thor Hanson

resourceful wood scavenging pays dividends with long burning coals as the night quickly turns bitter.

It is so cold that breathing hurts. The air is icy. Each inhalation crystallizes my air passages, right down to my lungs. The moon becomes a comforting friend as I consider my good fortune. Far different from the realities of that other world, whose limitations become more clear with each passing day, this experience truly strengthens me.

I awaken in darkness, sprawled in bear grass. It is as frigid a night in the woods as I can ever recall. The frost from my breath decorates my eyelids and chin, creating a mask to ward off the cold. My legs ache, and I know how old I am, lying there with a fist of chilled air against my body.

Part of my preparation is psyching myself up for any kind of weather. Around forty percent of body heat emanates from the head and extremities. If it is biting cold, I wear every polypropylene layer I have, add a wool hat, lightweight balaclava, mittens, a Gore-Tex hooded-windbreaker, and a second pair of polypro socks. During the day I secure one pair of the latter to my fanny pack in order to dry them out. I wear plastic bags under my socks, as vapor barrier liners, to battle the chilling numbness and warm my body core. At night I build a fire, crawl into my ultralight bivy sack, and sleep next to the red hot coals.

At higher altitudes, I find I can increase core warmth by placing pine needles and cattails inside my jacket, adding the same under my bivy for extra insulation, then sleeping on one side in a fetal position. What is under me becomes more crucial than what is over me.

I prefer conquering the higher passes by early afternoon to out-hustle late-day sudden storms. If one is coming, I would cover my head, hands, and neck with wool-derivative clothing. Cotton and down are useless when wet. When one allows cold, wind-whipped rain to run down your neck and back, one loses body heat appreciably faster.

I am alert for any extremity tingling that might signal marginal frost-bite. Sometimes I use a skin-tight trash bag as a magic undershirt for added warmth, and position a second one over the hip pack to protect its contents from the elements. I try to keep at least two polypropylene items dry by storing them individually zip-locked in plastic inside the pack. At night I place both shoes in protective bags, after warming them by the fire, to keep them supple and thawed at dawn.

Gore-Tex foul-weather gear is not guaranteed to be a winner when it comes to breathability, but it sure makes some miserable situations bearable. If the skies spray enough havoc, I would scurry for refuge, then switch to dry garb. I never hesitate to sit out one of these showstoppers; the danger of hypothermia or lightning found me taking the safer route.

Eventually, when excruciating fatigue finally overcomes air temperature trauma, I'm able to nod off.

Day 39 - August 17.   Sunrise finds me grateful for warmth and I let it embrace me. I look forward to a comparatively subdued trek over Mather Pass to Grouse Meadow. I celebrate the run with Bodyfuel, PowerBars, trail mix, dried fruit, and a nap near an unnamed lakelet.

At noon in an icy creek that's little more than a trickle, I wash my feet and socks. When my bare toes land on a fertile field of clover, it is a greater reward than I can imagine. I knead my toes in the soft carpet again and again. I never tire of this eerie sensation of simultaneous cold and warmth. I could remain here forever, letting the clover grow up to surround me in a cocoon of green velvet.

This floral sanctuary is surrounded by pristine lakes, gently flowing rivers, and the mild activity of the marshes. The wild summer berries and lichen-stained rocks provide a depth of contrast to humble the most perceptive artist. I listen breathlessly for the precious mountain melodies that occasionally interrupt the silence. A friendly raven provides company. A halo circles the sun and I am in high spirits. This sub-alpine beauty is as close as I will ever be to the Garden of Eden in this life.

Bliss is followed by remarkable contrast as I tax every sinew in a grunting hurdle over the "Golden Staircase." This masochistic artery was the final segment of the trail within the Sierra. I think about an Indian or early pioneer coming across this difficult but magnificent canyon for the first time, before the path was easily negotiated, perhaps at the end of a hard day.

There is not one iota of visible dirt on the trail, just the shards of knife-like granite that punish the balls and heels of both feet. Sharp pain intensifies into a steady dull ache on traumatic, brutal descents. I manage to limp through the rocky maze, groaning and wincing, as a strong crosswind finds me listing to the starboard side. An hour later I drop into a snow-fed swimming hole to minimize the searing trauma in my quadriceps. Before long I am hyperventilating trying to deal with the water's shock. I'm relegated to choosing one source of pain or the other.

Two miles later I round a sharp turn and nearly run into Doug Oliver. Doug flew in from the East Coast to hike the Sierra. We camp together at sundown. Tonight's spectacle includes a series of high-speed chases along a sandbar by three does. After frolicking on our camp perimeter, the playful participants notice their audience, and visibly startled, exit with a blur.

Day 40 - August 18.   The following morning at the La Conte Back-country Ranger Station, I share a cold breakfast with Steve Knipper and Mary Beth Cook. These two Lone Pine friends, who both work (at this writing) in separate wilderness areas near Mt. Whitney, had virtually sprinted over Bishop Pass from South Lake with a vital supply cache. The three of us now carve out eight tenacious miles up to Muir Pass. This breathtaking high-country spine is named after John Muir, a man who had a spartan attitude and considerable personal grit. Climbing it requires a great deal of discipline. It is arguably the toughest alpine Sierra passage and has a great propensity for harboring summer storms.

We lunch at the 11,955-foot pass partially sheltered by a 50-year-old stone hut that offers hikers protection from bone-chilling wind, sudden lightning storms, and stinging hail.

Reflections multiply in dizzying array from our high granite viewpoint as we drink in the eternal beauty of Wanda, Sapphire, and Evolution lakes. The latter is one of the Sierra's most precious jewels. Renowned photographer Ansel Adams often highlighted it as part of John Muir's famous "Range of Light."

Forty days and over 700 miles. That's seven 100-milers as racing goes, but there's no comparison. By measurable standards, everything is going great. Preparation, patience, and prayer have paid off. I am grateful for safe passage. However, my present good fortune doesn't alleviate my anxieties for the future.

In terms of a choice of journeys, I am aware of the absurdity in this one. I flash back to the astonished faces of hometown non-running friends, close neighbors, and immediate family (especially my worried mom) when I announced my intentions — the dropped jaws, muffled chuckles, then the reactions of those who really understood. The latter are long-distance trail running compatriots with similar brain damage. They already knew I was crazy. Almost without exception, a smile would stretch slowly and light up their faces, followed by a understanding glance. As time went on, when my seriousness became evident, nearly everyone got caught up in the enormity of the run. Most would make a surprise gesture of future assistance. Oddly, many of the offers came at critical, remote locations.

These people have been incredibly unselfish, and the weather has been beautiful.

Looking back, I've been blessed with an abundance of crystal-clear days. I haven't encountered a drop of rain since the deluge at Big Bear. This is considered a drought year due to abnormally low precipitation. In previous backpacking stints in this area, I have been hit with heavy thunderstorms for as many as five days in a row. Backcountry rangers inform me that this is the driest of the past five Sierra summers.

I think about how much the mountains have meant to me, what they've done for me, and how strongly this fire has burned within. I am an entirely different person, reborn with a deeper sensitivity. I welcome more of this transition. I marvel at how many women do not fear change — perhaps because of their ability to accept several roles in life. As for myself, it is a revelation that I find personal growth and change so exciting. I feel mildly disappointed that I bucked the challenge in my younger years.

I look forward to what the coming weeks have to offer.

Cleansed by this lifestyle, I never seem to get sick. Spartan living agrees with me. I seek out things that are good for me on a daily basis. I

Pause at Selden Pass   by Thor Hanson

am far less stressed when meandering through a rural dreamland. Both my body and the weather are holding up beautifully.

At times my mind drifts back to the clutter and hurry of my urban hometown where instant gratification is the quest, and impatience washes over all things. There, it seems, an addictive fantasy prevails. People anticipate winning the lottery or scoring big in a lawsuit — anything to take them out of the day's drudgery. It is this mind-set that has pushed the puritan work ethic off the planet. With little effort I visualize the undisciplined, self-destructive types that I see so often in my hometown — gulping "shooters" and sucking on Marlboros. They apparently think nothing of pumping more nicotine into their already withered lungs.

On the trail my patience has grown. I have uncovered abilities I didn't know I had. Even on rest days it seems I can tolerate almost anything.

What I only suspected going into this venture is now clear. When I hesitate to test my passion, I miss out on a lot of living. A thick-skinned stubbornness guards my inner core that looks on convention as a benign enemy. This alternatively uplifting and humbling catharsis has slain all the old torments of my life. It is almost as if I pulled a trigger which in turn sent a serene laser light straight to my gut. Past episodes of bitterness are now dissolved. I never loved nature, other people, or myself more than at this moment.

Steve and Mary Beth prove to be fantastic companions. They camp with me in McClure Meadows, then run back out to civilization over Piute Pass in the morning.

Day 41 - August 19. First light sees me running solo on a short, sensible 15-miler to Muir Trail Ranch where I pick up a supply box. Once there, vacationing Thor Hanson insists I stay as his overnight guest. The ensuing conversation and a deep-dish vegetarian pizza warm my soul and stomach.

I earn my dinner at the ranch by giving a succinct dissertation on the run. My emotional expansions on daily mileage, gear simplicity, and trail encounters arouse bulging eyeballs from my listeners. They are a group of fairly sedentary enthusiasts from all walks of life. Not surprisingly, most of the questions center on how I survive and sleep warm enough with only a 15-pound pack.

Several ice-cold cervezas accompany our immersion in the 105-degree Trail Ranch hot springs. This fusion of external and internal therapy works magic on the mind, muscles, and inner spirit. Here at the ranch, cares disappear within this peaceful refuge. Hours of unbroken sleep follow.

Yosemite Bound

Day 42 - August 20. Thor paces me up to Selden Pass at midmorning. Along the way we divvy up brunch on a shimmering outdoor tapestry lined with lakelets that reflect myriad variations of turquoise and blue. A low-gliding raven with outstretched wings spirals round and round on the thermals that nudge a towering butte. This rugged setting is rimmed by a flawless purity. We anticipate what it will be like on the upper perimeter of this sub-alpine valley. We are soon rewarded with resplendent dabs of unspoiled fireweed, lupine, and Indian paintbrush.

I offer Thor a warm embrace of profound appreciation. We then bid adieu and eventually run down opposite sides of Selden Pass.

Big stands of pine flank a churning creek that knifes through glaciated bedrock, then spills over a tall, vertical shelf. This contrasting drama of U-shaped basin and rugged range highlights my quiet passage. The trail climbs moderately, then steeply, over a long, strenuous slope to a vista-laden plateau. I descend at a more comfortable pace by way of well-graded switchbacks down to Mono Creek and tonight's meadow camp.

A timid doe and two fawns barely observe my almost-naked arrival as they continue to nibble at streamside brush.

Day 43 - August 21. Sunrise initiates a rugged 30-miler over Silver Pass. Following the rugged ascent, I am looking forward to seeing a human or an animal as I've been alone for two-and-a-half hours. Several graceful llamas lead a slow-moving pack train headed for Purple Lake. When I question the choice of pack animals, the wrangler explains that four llamas eat about the same amount as one horse. They are decidedly more sure-footed, tolerate altitude better, and impart less damage to the trail. Their soft padded feet are much gentler than the shod hooves of a horse or mule. These furry sherpas project a sphinx-like appearance with their supple, periscoping necks and fluffy, pointed ears.

I bound upward toward sparkling Virginia Lake and Duck Pass Junction. It takes me almost three hours through dense red firs to reach Red's Meadow where I am met at the trailhead by hometown friends, John and Shirley Cosgrove. They are duly equipped with unlimited ice-cold beverages, and they provide stabilizing affection. John and Shirley drive me to their nearby Mammoth Lakes condo to soothe some well-thrashed quads in a therapeutic jacuzzi. I feel like I am on a euphoric flight through a fantasy land.

I show my heartfelt appreciation to my hosts after consuming three hot gourmet meals — all at the same sitting.

Days 44-45 - August 22-23. My stay prompted John to pen this note to his running club:

> *Can you imagine traversing over 800 miles in 43 days and arriving within five minutes of a pre-arranged time — without ever using a watch? The fact that I was stunned by this merely meant I didn't know Bob very well. His first*

words were: 'May I have a cold beer?' I was able to respond affirmatively and then observed a mountainous thirst in operation. . . . Bob's journey has taken him into the realm of the true wilderness man and has inspired and intrigued me so that I now try to run solely in the woods.

Day 46 - August 24. Following my second rest day, Southern California ultra-endurance athlete Carlos Arellanes drives in. He will share some high-altitude adventure on yet another 30-plus-miler, slicing the innards of Yosemite's matchless high country. A spirited send-off by the Cosgroves and local newspaper reporters fires up my after-burners. Amid the backslaps and handshakes, I even do an impromptu dance, bouncing and bobbing in the thin, crisp air.

The vertiginous climb winds along a spectacular sun-bleached adventure-land. Unique granite lakes nestle like magnificent gems in their cirques.

The famous knife-edge Minarets are shepherded by 13,157-foot Mount Ritter. Ritter is King of the Mountains in the Sierra's middle portion, a Shasta of the South and Whitney of the North. At a distance of less than 3,000 feet from its summit, you may find tributaries of the San Joaquin River bursting forth from the icy snow of the glaciers that load its flanks. Slightly beyond are found the highest tributaries of the Tuolumne and the Merced. Thus, the fountains of three principal rivers in California are within a radius of less than ten miles.

Leaving this sanctuary, we catapult over Donohue Pass into an expansive stadium of creeks and lakes. Noisy cascades muscle their turbulence into spirit-cleansing grottoes as we lean toward Tuolumne Meadows. The tangy scent of pine dominates the timbered lowlands. Tiny cones carpet the springy tapestry, crunching underfoot like popcorn kernels.

Russ Melanson, perennial finisher of the Western States 100-Mile Trail Race, runs out to greet us with water, high energy bars, and a big grin. Due to the prevailing horse traffic, we refrain from quenching our considerable thirst at river crossings.

Carlos is awed by the many vibrant contrasts superimposed within this primitive arena. We drink in the colors, letting our minds spin free with running's sharp pleasures. Fair and foul scents leap from crannies and corners until you pay them attention. I'm sweating like an open faucet. The day's perfect marriage of scenic intoxication and exhausted bliss culminates with a hot meal in the rustic Tuolumne Meadows Lodge.

Ever aware of the huge difference running has made in my life, I am not surprised when I hear the same from others. Russ, now in his mid-50s and preparing for retirement in Foresthill, California, has spent over three decades with the fire service. He is (at this writing) a Fire Marshal in Los Angeles. Like C.H.P. Officer Fred Hermann from Lancaster, Russ had begun to see stress taking its toll and was searching for a means of turning that process around. Running has saved his sanity. Intrigued by my venture, Russ also commits to a second stint during my third summer, just south of Snoqualmie Pass in Washington. Russ will drive some 1,300 miles each way — just to share a day and a few meals.

As Russ puts it:

There's something about an adventure of this magnitude that makes you want to experience it — at least in part. I'm not content to be an armchair traveler. Although I would only be spending a couple of days with Bob, I had a sense of the true excitement I'd feel just being there, and I wanted that as a part of my life.

In much the same way that running has added a new circle of friends to my life and a tremendous sense of satisfaction that comes from knowing these old, tired bones can still keep up, I wanted the added dimension this journey would bring. Though Bob was astounded by the offers of support he received from so many, it didn't really surprise me — we all want to be part of this terrific accomplishment.

A snug pack aids in perfecting balance   Lee Freeman

4 We Did It

*The weakest among us can become some kind of athlete,
but only the strongest can survive as spectators. Only the
hardiest can withstand the perils of inertia, inactivity and
immobility. . . . From the moment you become a spectator,
everything is downhill. It's a life that ends before the
cheering and the shouting die.*

— George Sheehan
the "Running Cardiologist"

The Toughest Days of Summer

Day 47 - August 25. Following the farewells, I head northward alone,
skirting a stirring necklace of waterfalls and shimmering pools. I appre-
hensively dip into one near Glen Aulin and sunbathe on a slippery granite
slab.

Today's climb circumvents massive, steep-hanging canyons carved by
ancient glaciers. A cool breeze softens the sun's intense rays as I stop
periodically to wet my brow, hat, and bandanna from mirror-like sheets of
water. A restful micro-climate of moss and man-sized ferns line the roof
of a rock overhang where I break for lunch.

Diverse textures abound within this land of jagged ridges, bone-col-
ored basins, and noisy chutes as I move giddily toward camp. Five curious
deer stare at this lightly-clad human intruder throughout the rich evening
hours. A glittering tapestry surrounds Matterhorn Junction, so named for
the nearby peak's similarity to the "original" in Switzerland.

Day 48 - August 26 This 26-miler will take three hours longer than
a subsequent 28. This is the most hellish stint since the border. I tackle
five passes — two of them unnamed — in 13 hours. Seavey Pass proves
the steepest, abounding with jagged rocks strewn over a staircase-like
trail. The downhill side is so cruel that each delicate step requires several
seconds. Sharp rocks press their teeth into the insoles of my shoes. This
physiological torture creates a lactic inferno inside my body.

Due to ground-level eye concentration needed to traverse this section,
the metal Pacific Crest Trail markers are stapled only inches from the tree
bottoms for visibility.

Swimming in Benson Lake and basking on a sandy beach soften the
journey. The day's toll is apparent, however, by my scratchy throat,
throbbing quads, and the war going on inside my aching cranium.

In contrast to the meals of the past week, tonight's dinner of two
PowerBars and some dried fruit seems meager indeed. But the setting —

a pampering fire, a moonlit night, and a powdery sand bed — compensates. The temperature drops below 30 degrees, which jolts me into a drill-like shudder after my return from a nature call. At this moment, a few thin layers are all that shield me from this wild land's chills. I grunt out a few philosophical ramblings that border on weirdness, then finally drift off into nocturnal oblivion.

Day 49 - August 27.   I set out at dawn to take advantage of the cool morning hours, then cruise rapidly through a series of flat sections. After leap-frogging over Dorothy and Leavitt passes, I pick up blustery headwinds and 40-degree temperatures just south of 9,624-foot Sonora Pass. It is a chore to maintain forward momentum, much less keep my equilibrium. My efforts to do so are frustratingly feeble. I look like a frightened fly on the edge of a bowl as I wobbly negotiate unstable pumice and chipped shale.

The chill factor is brutal. The air is frigid. Flurries of small debris driven on 60-mile-per-hour winds — as I traverse a seven-mile-long volcanic ledge — dig into my skin like thousands of tiny, sharp needles. I wear every layer in my pack: two garbage bags, the Gore-Tex windbreaker, and three polypro shirts comprise the protective barricades. Sharp rocks

60 mph winds at 10,000 feet on narrow ledge   by Mike Dirham

First hot meal of the week at Sonora Pass   by Kim Chapman

torture my already sensitive blisters on one heel and three toes. A now-tilted skeletal machine, I begin to list even more appreciably to one side. My legs tremble, but somehow my nerve holds on. I feel like I have a mid-air toehold on a high wire trail with no safety net.

At this point I have been alone for three days. Now I am completely out of food. I mentally pry myself open to reach for a stabilizing handle on all this. Adrenalin rushes through me.

Excitement mounts when help arrives. I spot veteran ultrarunners and wiry, congenial Redwood City firemen, Gary Belanger and Slick Chapman, just south of Sonora Pass. These longtime friends have just driven four hours with their better halves, Katie and Kim.

At Sonora Pass, I feast on array of gourmet delights that seem so out of place in this stark setting. As I devour the meal, I fight to exhibit more civilized table manners than my voracious appetite threatens to overwhelm.

All around me, the multifaceted arena oozes with richness. One of my lifetime goals has been to spend as many waking hours as possible in the outdoors. With the intensity of the weather and the fear of hunger now gone, I am able to get back in touch with these positive feelings. I am intensely aware that the potential for danger threatens every thought and permeates every fiber — a few hours ago it was all I could do to manage the present, much less consider the future.

Day 50 - August 28. Spent a leisurely rest day at nearby Chipmunk Flat for extensive map study.

Day 51 - August 29.   I head back out for a solo venture through the pristine glades between Wolf Creek Saddle and Asa Lake. Amid trailhead whoops and hollers from Slick's bellowing voicebox, the good-hearted Belanger duo shadow me for an hour, embrace me, and then turn back toward civilization.

Civilization. What an odd concept that seems to me now, as if the whole concept is reversed. Are cars, high-rises, and the constant drone of television truly indicative of civilization? Compared to what I'm experiencing now, all of that seems decidedly backward. Despite nature's inherent propensity for causing disaster, she is on the whole, quite civilized. A code prevails among her inhabitants, and although in this survival-of-the-fittest world there is sometimes violence, it doesn't appear as ultimately destructive as the violence that prevails in our urban world.

I turn my thoughts to the trail ahead. The sun casts a warm glow, birds chirp, twigs crackle underfoot, and my senses are flooded with the beauty of the land. As an underdressed zealot, I exult in the priceless joy of self-propulsion within a forest calm.

I pass the rib bones of a mule deer skeleton, bare but not yet decayed. Cracked and picked over, it is a clean, tidy demise. Nothing wasted.

Legible mileage signs, supplemented by metallic silver diamonds or green trail emblems on wood posts, are a welcome sight. There have been so many nebulous intersections in the past weeks, with no marking whatsoever. This section of the trail showcases the most meticulously manicured surface I have seen in 51 days.

A sore instep tendon is aggravated by the mega-miles, but midday immersion in a cascading waterfall brings relief.

I am sharing the trail tread now with a small group of hefty cows. A burst of vigorous hand clapping moves them off the path and down a gully. I am alone once again, as I drop down to Ebbetts Pass for a lonely makeshift bivouac.

Day 52 - August 30.   The sky is the darkest it has been in a month. The wind howls, creating an echo. It is brutally cold as I hitch a morning ride down the spindly artery to Markleeville. Neighboring Grover Hot Springs helps relax taut muscles, and topnotch ultradistance runner Jim Drake and gourmet trail chef Tom Fish bring in fresh fruit and vegetables for tonight's meal in this idyllic setting.

Afterwards, I reflect on my chosen lifestyle. It has now become clear who I am, where I want to go, and the steps I must take to get there.

Day 53 - August 31.   Jim Drake and I traverse a grueling 27 miles of alpine landscape from Ebbetts Pass to Carson Pass in 10 hours. Worsening snow flurries on perilous ridges whip us relentlessly. We hop over mammoth boulders, fractured rubble from unstable cliffside walls, then wade through murky bogs. We are conscious of the impact these conditions would have on someone traveling with a heavy load — such as hikers with heavy, cumbersome backpacks. Doubtless they would have an incredibly difficult time just managing forward motion, compared to the markedly less cumbersome hip packs we're sporting. Even when running on all cylinders with minimal weight, this is no place to try to make good time.

The path is bordered with sheer vertical drops. It seems as if we're always running toward a summit. Because of this summer's drought and lack of stream flows, we carry plenty of liquid. I wear protective (ultra-violet ray-blocking) sunglasses with glare-resistant shades and leather side-guards.

The day is capped with an epicurean delight, courtesy of Tom. It's a feast worthy of a disciplined runner: vegetarian lasagna, salad, and fruit. There are no cheering throngs this evening, but our own hearts lift, spirits soaring.

Day 54 - September 1. The next day's dawn betrays us from the onset as we warily skirt narrow serpentine valleys through bombardments of rain, hail, and menacing winds. We can hardly complain, though; this basin is sorely in need of saturation, as evidenced by the rapidly browning meadows and the fire danger.

When we arrive at Highway 50, just southwest of Lake Tahoe, the roar of fast-moving holiday traffic drums like an artillery onslaught. A house-length motorhome comes into view. Clearly its owners have come to conquer the wilderness. The folding chairs and green, artificial turf rug strapped to the roof seem absurdly out of place. We cross the road as if in a trance and amble into the tiny settlement of Little Norway (now burned down).

Day 55 - September 2. It is Labor Day weekend. I spend part of it in a fitting endeavor, scrubbing dirty toilets in exchange for meals and a mattress at a church camp by Echo Lake.

I Want To Go Home

Day 56 - September 3. Trail specialist Jim King, one of this country's top ultramarathoners and three-time winner of the Western States 100-Miler, paces me over Dick's Pass into the spectacular Velma Lakes paradise. We are now in the heart of the expansive Desolation Wilderness, a forested alpine arena studded with over 50 lakes and well rimmed by a myriad of peaks.

In addition to Jim's multitudinous achievements, he is one of the finest human beings I have met in this lifetime, so his company is always an honor. Jim is a "rep" for a major running firm and a strong spiritual person. Our friendship extends back over many past races. His humble demeanor and gracious personal warmth set an impeccable example for us all. He is a winner in every category.

It proves to be the longest, coldest, and wettest day of the run. Being a scantily clad trailblazer in bad weather is less than satisfying. Whether caused by rain, snow, or your own perspiration, dampness on unprotected skin can drain you of heat faster than a howling blast of arctic wind. In these conditions, an immobilizing injury can quickly prove disastrous. If you are wet and incapacitated, your body temperature will drop. This is usually followed by shivering, a loss of coordination, and ultimately, unconsciousness.

From a safer vantage point, I might enjoy the resplendent rainbow silhouettes and the frenzied spectacle of discharging electricity on a distant cliff. However, right now I feel my hair standing on end. With the thunderclaps rolling and echoing among the peaks, I am at the mercy of the weather gods.

Although this day would have been tough enough as a pre-planned 24-miler, it ends up being a torturous 31. The additional miles result from a torn-up dirt road that prevents Jim's wife, Tina, from reaching us with necessary supplies. We are forced to run almost to the west shore of Lake Tahoe.

I spend the night at Squaw Valley with Jim and Tina, feeling ever grateful for their camaraderie and the warm, dry surroundings.

Days 57 - September 4. Only two days remain to Donner Pass. On the first of these, I cover 18 miles from Barker Pass to just north of Granite Chief — with a side trip to Five Lakes Basin for lunch and a therapeutic foot bath. Throughout the day I am slipping on wet weeds, hopscotching over broken cobbles, and dodging deep holes.

It is the fifth straight day of strong winds, rain, and extreme cold. After a summer of drought, it appears that an early fall has been ordered by Mother Nature as compensation. Near Mountain Meadow Lake, a connecting trail permits a drenched descent back to Squaw Valley.

Tasting the Nectar

Day 58 - September 5. The relaxed setting at Squaw Valley provides much needed emotional renewal. Suddenly, I realize it is Day 58 — the culmination of 1,055 miles on the Pacific Crest Trail. Looking back, I feel as if I have been running through a zoo without fences — surrounded on all sides by a gargantuan botanical garden.

Leaving the kindredship of the King duo behind, I commence a long arduous haul back to the main artery.

Amidst pensive images of primal stillness between Tinkers Knob and Mt. Lincoln, something comes alive within me and I weep openly. The last day of the first summer brings release of tremendous joy and spiritual fulfillment. I weave like a moving stick-shadow toward California Highway Patrol Officer Bruce Mauldin (a premier ultradistance runner). He will be my sole greeting party at Donner Summit.

Carboloading high in the Sierra Nevada   by Bob Carpenter

In cartoon-like fashion, I dart speedily into the belly of each switch-backing turn, a doubled fist pumping the air for emphasis. Arms that just two weeks ago moved as if covered with cement, today glide like kite sticks through the dense tangles of splintered, weatherbeaten pines. I move effortlessly over the brown sward, blowing occasional steam rings into the austere landscape. I can hear the expelled air bursting from my lungs with long, clean exertion. I surge into the home stretch with new life, fresh strength, and an absence of pain. The sweat-caked tears continue to well as I fly with pounding heart into Bruce's warm embrace. My dreams rise up to meet the moment. On a nearby rock, a single ice-cold beer awaits me.

Nurturing Nostalgia

The wet liquid liberates enough brain cells to allow some stark realiz-ations to hit home: I have just traversed close to a 200,000 feet in elevation change, averaging around 24 miles a day for 45 running days. Looking down at my still quivering legs, I shake my head in disbelief at the truly remarkable machine God has created in the human body.

Bruce drives me to his home in Auburn for two days of blissful unwinding. The contemplation that will rule my thoughts in the months ahead finds me recognizing that this intoxicating connection with nature, while immeasurably rewarding, has depleted me.

Many 12-hour days were spent on unpredictable trail, some of it virtually falling away from lack of repair. A careless mistake could have plummeted me down a mountain side — possibly into history. In precarious situations, I have been 100-percent exposed to the elements. Spiritual strength and determination have led me through countless challenging encounters with nature. One-on-one with God's creation, I got to know myself rapidly, in a way I had never fully known myself before. There is no buffer zone between me and my feelings, no true means of escaping the awareness I now possess — no way out, or back. My daily act of giving thanks for safe passage now seems a small gesture for such a large reward. Despite occasional low points, I never once considered throwing in the towel.

I have experienced a whole new social system. Rural towns and tiny resorts are a welcome breather — instead of the other way around, as people seeking only creature comforts might view them. I have developed a depth of simplicity and a sincere appreciation for the barest shelter. My cravings for hot meals often loomed as large as a movie screen and were inescapable. So was my pervasive desire for human company. The exquisiteness of the senses — of smell and hearing and sight — that I never could have known before this journey, kept me awestruck throughout its duration.

The daily absence of concrete, pollution, cars, phones, clocks, and urban rules was an ecstasy of another realm. With each new territory I covered, I felt like a solitary spirit darting out of the shadows. I moved quickly and quietly through the wilderness, leaving behind only clean footstrikes. I figuratively scratched the underbelly of the clouds, gleaming with them in my own inner peace.

Hometown writer Paul Walker touched on this premier summer with these words:

> We all have dreams. But how many of us have the conviction to bridge the gap between idea and reality, yet the strength to succeed?

My ageless mother, an exuberant, beautiful human being, has been a key influence in this run. Always a source of inspiration, she wrote these 15 simple words which have carried me in more ways than she can imagine:

Thousands of miles of footprints pursuing the pleasures, perils, excitement, and peace of elevated places!

Summer of '86
Donner Pass to the
Columbia River Gorge

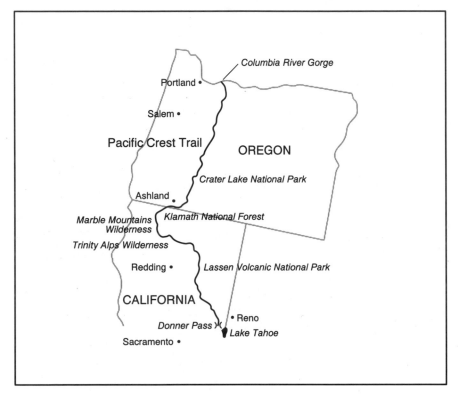

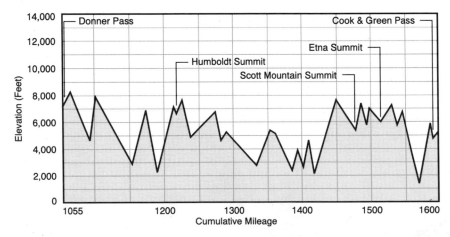

A moment's rest high above an alpine lake   by Lee Freeman

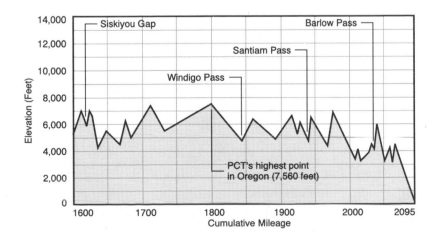

One step of four-and-one-half million   by Bob Carpenter

5 An Endless Hip-Bruiser _____

*Life is just too easy. Society is so cushioned that we have
no opportunity for struggle. People are bred to struggle.
We need to express that or else be incomplete.*

— Gordon Ainsleigh
Founder of Western States 100-Mile Endurance Run

After enduring ten comparatively mundane months as a high school
physical education teacher, I return to northern California to crew for
fellow ultrarunner Jan Levet in the annual Western States 100-Miler. Then,
I spend one week training in the heat and at altitude, during which I run
up to five hours a day on tough trails in 95-degree heat. I spend the
evenings in Auburn — long a hotbed for trail running enthusiasts — with
Bruce Mauldin who welcomed me as I collared last summer. Despite my
growing enthusiasm, I begin to sense the anxiety creeping in as I get closer
to shunning the comforts and complexities of a home base.

Route Difficulty

Day 59 - July 5, 1986. I set out from Donner Pass, the exact spot
where I completed the 1,055th mile the summer before, with supportive,
hometown friend Ted Zimbelman and veteran ultrarunner Nancy Taylor
from Auburn. Today they will push me through 30 miles, half of them over
a myriad of ice patches. The trail is obliterated by debris from late spring
storms. It has been a fairly wet winter, and trail passage will be hazardous
for at least another two weeks. In some spots we plunge up to our hips in
snow drifts, our breaths condensing in steam-like puffs, a chilly contrast
to the balmy 60-degree air. Most of the morning I wear a protective
Gore-Tex shell over my mittens and thick plastic bags over my socks,
inside my shoes. The hushed, quiet, moisture-laden trees and snow blanketed purity of the landscape are exhilarating. I begin to feel at home once
again.

Struggling over this terrain is a supreme task. With full water bottles,
we hunker down over Castle Pass to Jackson Meadow Reservoir. Frequent
landmarks, the sun's location, and a trusty compass help us get back on
track when we lose the trail three times in two hours. We encounter a solo
hiker sitting under a thick canopy of pine. He proudly shows us his
backcountry diet for the trek — several hundred dried anchovy fishheads
and unshelled peanuts intermingled in a large, double-layered plastic bag.

We are elated when we discover a snow-free, tailored trail in Bear
Valley where the path is well graded on cushioned pine needles. My ankles
and quads are screaming with delight at the therapeutic diversion from

toe-grabbing roots and eroded ruts encountered earlier that day. The sky is blue, open meadows flank sparkling lake basins, and the earth smells of fresh clay. Suddenly, it seems a new world where no one has passed before me.

As part of a personal practice that I have developed over the years, I prefer not to talk in a quiet mountain setting unless something significant needs to be said. I sometimes have to explain this tactfully to supportive friends. The greater anticipation of the beauty and its enchantment occurs more readily when the atmosphere isn't spoiled by meaningless banter. However, unless you're of hermit mentality, the interaction of human companionship creates a harmonious balance. Sharing the journey with a compatible friend halves any unforeseen misery and can double the commensurate joy of a wild and remote land.

Even in silence, teamwork is essential. If an accompanying friend and I became separated due to varying speeds, we would take turns making rock or stick arrows at trail forks. The trailing runner then removes them, restoring the tread to its natural pristine state. This usually prevents wrong turns due to confusing junctions or fatigue.

When we reach the noisy reservoir, Nevada City resident Rick Maltin, a close friend of Ted Zimbelman, shuttles Nancy and Ted back to Donner Pass. I will now be without a pacer for over a week. I will try not to let today's company spoil me. Ted returns home in such a highly motivated state that he writes Congress to petition that a section of the trail be renamed after me.

Day 60 - July 6.   Dawn has me striking out to the Highway 49 crossing above Wild Plum Campground near Sierra City. The morning breezes propel the trees into a slow, silent dance. The warming sun divides its presence by leaving clean, bright spots on the forested carpet and long shafts of light on the canyon walls.

As on other mornings in this quiet kingdom, I can hear my heart pounding in my ears. A profound peace takes me into its arms and won't let me go. With each deep breath I can feel the warmth come down around me.

How odd it is to be a constantly moving visitor in a very private place. I pause momentarily to determine whether someone can hear me. I get the feeling I am never completely alone. I almost visualize someone breathing over my shoulder, and although I tell myself no one is there, I turn to look anyway. How minuscule I feel in this encircling forest of peering eyes.

At my own home in Southern California's perennially crowded Manhattan Beach, there is so little quiet and so few stars. I consider the absurdity of people vying for parking spots and the psychic energy that it sucks from them — in contrast to this place where I might go thirty miles seeing hardly anyone. On the trail there is a feeling of elemental self-awareness — an actual freeing of and from the body — that can best be produced through rhythmic, strenuous activity.

It is difficult to express what I cannot see but can only feel. I crave these long, hard moments free of dream.

Rick Maltin is so overwhelmed by the run's aura that he drives over 50 miles back to offer encouragement as I amble into Sierra City. After sharing a chat and an ice-cold brew on a country store porch, he departs at dusk. The small portion of spicy chili I consume does calisthenics in my gut. It also reminds me that I am about to return to solo trekking and the absence of commiseration.

The Sierra City Post Office, which houses my trail package, doesn't open until 9:30 a.m. One needs an early departure on high-mileage days. Resupply delays can throw off a preferred schedule. Also, many village postal operations close at 4:00 p.m. Any difficulties preventing smooth passage during the day might back up your arrival until dusk, too late to claim your package.

While having a hearty meal at the Sierra Buttes Inn, I am so enthralled with the infectious camaraderie that I decide to stay as a transient guest. The entire town treats me as a sort of prodigal son. They make me feel like an integral part of them.

Day 61 - July 7.   After a shave, two glorious showers sandwiched around a good night's respite, map study, foot care, journal writing, and a self-inflicted haircut, I have lunch with a temporary resident of Sierra City. He has hiked part of both the Appalachian and Continental Divide trails. Today's rest day is inspirational as well as entertaining.

In many settlements along the route I jot down uplifting anecdotes in a special Pacific Crest Trail register. I also glean the tales of others. One "signee," Southern California resident Terry Hartig, lost all of his toes in the Sierra spring of 1983 due to frostbite. Three years later he is now back on the trail hiking, three weeks ahead of me.

One hiker who was on the trail for a goodly duration wrote this in the small-town register:

> *I own the smelliest breath, the ugliest dog, and the mean-*
> *est woman. I can outhike and outfart any living creature.*
> *I 'are' a mountain man.*

Some days the abbreviation PCT stands for "Pretty Crummy Trail." However, I have my own version of that acronym: "Patience, Character, and Tenacity." It will take all three to get where I want to go.

Heavenly Lonesomeness

Day 62 - July 8.   Dawn's golden light paints the surrounding arena of towering massifs with a warm shepherding glow. The endless phalanx of mountain sanctuaries splashes my soul with nourishing rhythms of purity.

Duly pumped up, I crank upward through shoelace-yanking thornbushes, along ridges with rocks the size of refrigerators, toward the 8,550-foot Sierra Buttes fire lookout. Today I will run a thirteen-and-a-half hour, rattlesnake-punctuated 32 miles to Nelson Creek.

Five miles out at a trickling spring, I spot a huge rattler waiting motionless with infinite patience. It appears to be stalking an unguarded rodent as it anticipates that inevitable mortality of crossed paths. My next glance illustrates my error as partway down the reptile's body there appears a tumor-like bulge, about the size of a large frog or chipmunk. In its digestive sequence, the snake gears down to sluggish behavior, evidently having difficulty recrossing the tiny rivulet toward its shady den to snooze off the meal.

The snake pauses momentarily, neck darting back and forth, as if suspended from a guidewire. I kick some trail dirt with the edge of a running shoe and am rewarded when the snake makes a quick exit. In the next half hour, two more rattlers skitter off the narrow tread when they hear my arrival. I sharpen my concentration to the utmost.

North of the fire lookout, I use the lower elevation Pacific Crest Trail alternate route which affords drinking water, swim stops, and a brilliant sapphire kingdom. Rich scents of verdant flora drift among the fractured flanks of gargantuan peaks. I am color drunk on the primal purity of a lonesome, rugged place.

I round a sharp bend and run into the rear flank of a large group of camp counselors. When I tell them I am going to Canada they respond with inspirational serenades and a spontaneous ovation. The spirited hand-slapping, along with their sheer size in numbers (reminding me of similar moving moments at the girls camp near Wrightwood), has me weeping unashamedly with joy.

A few stare in disbelief at my battered fanny pack, now held together with duct tape and restitching. After 15 minutes of verbal camaraderie, my passage is humorously permitted only after the entire group runs along beside me for 300 yards. Then they divide themselves equally to create a funnel-like chute and I run between them, surrounded by rousing cheers.

This event reaffirms my penchant for outdoor life and reminds me of the greater graces of showing character, rather than just being one.

Midday brings a munch-stop at Packer Lake, a cooling dip in Deer Lake, followed by a backbreaking climb up to the main trail. I reach a newly built segment that has aimless convolutions through every contour and gully. Although the path is in great condition for running, there are no usable campsites or springs. I continue wearily on into the dusk hoping to find a decent flat area.

I encounter two large, slick ice patches that block my route just before dark. I skirt them by climbing, on all fours, high up a fragile bank. A sheet of treacherous ice covers the denuded soil and rocks. Internal butterflies massage my nerve endings raw with fear. I frantically search for stable mini-ledges to sink in a fingernail, zipper of my Gore-Tex jacket, or a corner tooth — anything to help me claw my way along.

For me, off-trail bushwhacking is a familiar rite of passage. A hometown ritual of near-daily pushups pays off as I muscle up the precarious slope, then scamper above the two icy areas.

The second one finds me shuddering as I think of my close friend who died in similar conditions. A plummet into either ice chute could possibly take my own life. A crash-landing into a tree or properly angled boulder might be my only salvation, should I be collared by the gravest reprimand Mother Nature could dish out. This setting resembles an Olympic downhill ski run without the well-groomed, safe, level finish area at the bottom.

I somberly descend back to the trail. I am drained emotionally and fatigued from the struggle with snow and ice. I find myself yearning for the scorching heat that seemed so inhospitable at this point last summer. A couple of surprise, four-point landings act as my frustrating grand finale. It is now so dark I cannot see more than 50 feet. The thrashing I have taken has depleted an already precariously low fuel tank.

Wedged in at 45 degrees for the night   by Mike Dirham

Clattering tufted woodpeckers and a dozen passing deer take me out of my misery and brighten the evening. I will sleep in a hastily devised and rudely angled bedroom. I wedge my bivy into the 45-degree mountain slope using a large granite slab for my headboard and two fallen, rotting logs as foot braces. I toss fitfully most of the night despite the day's fatigue.

> *However mean your life is, meet it and live it; Do not shun it and call it hard names. It is not so bad as you are. It looks poorest when you are richest. The fault-finder will find faults even in paradise.*

> — Henry Thoreau

When Running Hurts

Day 63 - July 9. Morning light initiates a quad-thrashing 26-miler to the Middle Fork of the Feather River. The largest suspension bridge on the entire Pacific Crest Trail awaits at the canyon bottom. Downright cruel terrain becomes one flagging ordeal: hot, boring, and waterless.

The mindless Fowler Peak segment is little more than a rutted fire road. No one has gone to the trouble of constructing an aesthetically appealing trail alongside it.

My footing is abominable as I approach the roaring river. The precariously narrow single track slaloms down steep talus through a myriad of large boulders and intertwined brush. Large leaves obscure ankle-wrenching loose stones. This disconcerting real estate also comes packaged with inhospitable upgrades. My pack is getting cumbersome and cutting into my hips on both sides.

Prevention of debilitating injury is a constant challenge. I instantly switch my weight to my upslope foot when a badly angled slope forces me to lean out over a sheer drop. My outside foot thrusts me forward in a shuffling posture like a guiding rudder. Bending my legs lowers my buttocks and creates a more stable center of gravity. Pummeled quads now absorb the brunt of the impact.

My downslope foot is severely pronated and straining my achilles tendon. To compensate, I do extra stretching and add a heel lift to that shoe.

I am now forced to interrupt this tortuous descent to lance a nasty, nut-sized blister, which is perfectly rimmed by cracking skin, on the ball of my foot. I remove a loose portion of the covering sheath, leaving raw flesh that will require clean bandages and moleskin daily. For the next two weeks I will run with three traumatized toes and minimal protective padding under them.

By the end of this summer the second toe on my right foot will be dislocated and lean over the top of the big toe. This unsightly scenario is caused by a mismatched pair of shoes (size ten left and nine right) and the cumulative impact of long downhills that forcibly bend that one append-age. I'm unable to cut an opening across the smaller shoe's toe-box due to the abundance of trail debris.

It is apparent that no runner on a wild country sabbatical need seek out pain. It will eventually surface on its own.

It may take ambition to be "someone," but it takes courage to be yourself. Your dreams are on the line. I think how nature magnifies your weaknesses as I scream at a couple of jagged rocks. Just keeping my head matters more than muscle and running tenacity.

To offset the sapping rigors, I take purposeful pauses to savor lake vistas that reflect numerous shades of blue.

It is tough at times to determine what I yearn for most — a shower, shave, shampoo, and towel; the constitution of a longshoreman; or companionship. How fragile we all are. When the need to be touched diminishes the benefits of aloneness, strength can be hard to come by. Faith and doubt seem to be taking turns, like breathing in and out, as I reach for my physical and moral limits during this quest toward my own "absolute."

The evenings offer a genuine stillness that reaffirms my presence. It is hard to witness a more brilliant Sierra sky than when the moon is still hidden and my small evening fire is extinguished. When it turns bitter cold, the mosquito population becomes immobile as well. It takes little to put me in a contemplative state — the tinkling of hot coals, the stellar illumination of a constellation, or a spindle-like crag punctuating a flawless, outdoor cathedral.

Each day's recovery from the cumulative effect of back-to-back quad-pounding runs brings its own sort of jubilation. I learn to respect the subtle difference between trail impact and trail texture. When my shoe's midsole life wanes, I add cushioning inserts. Despite this diligence, I pick up nagging stone bruises that create needle-sharp twinges. Frigid baths in streams combined with oral anti-inflammatories offset a disproportionate amount of this maddening, downhill-accentuated trauma.

I would use three pairs of New Balance shoes each summer, one about every 15 running days, because of trail irregularity and rubble. I am counting on the new shoes to offer insurance against catastrophic, trip-aborting injury for the 156 days I'm on the trail, and today is number 63. This will be the longest summer, it will encompass some of the worst trail, and I will incur the most physical problems.

Tonight's sandbar dinner table features granola, dried fruit, nuts, and water. Right now I would kill for some hot vegetarian lasagna and a 30-minute massage. It is such an effort to dissuade my negativity that I nearly forgo the giant light show above, singing its sparkling melody.

Day 64 - July 10. The morning brings a searing traverse of Bear Canyon, culminating with a seven-mile, 2,700-foot climb to Lookout Rock. By nightfall I will have covered 116 miles in five days.

North of the lookout stately pines stand together in remarkable tranquility. I reverse my gaze to drink in the unobstructed view of Sierra Buttes.

My passage through unblemished land, an altar of austere perfection, fosters a moral renewal. It is almost as if a window to eternity had burst open and unleashed the wonders of a personalized paradise. Worldly hurts seem to disappear within this thicket of purified soul. The silence of the mountains and guardianship from the heavens are the best love affair.

Today's most disheartening episode occurs when I place my fanny pack next to some trail-side bushes during a rest. After strapping it on, I develop a relentless itch, later followed by a badly festered case of poison oak.

With Spanish Peak looming just ahead, I hobble down to Bucks Lake store for kippered herring, a cold drink, and 48 hours at the home of ultrarunner Jerry Blinn in nearby Quincy.

Days 65-66 - July 11-12. I know Jerry through a number of long distance trail races. After replenishing foot cream, lip ice, gorp, Power-Bars, and dried fruit, I treat the ugly nodules that have toxified my rib cage with prednisone and hydrocortisone cream. I am not the most cheerful guest at Jerry's son's birthday party. I opt for comic relief by revving up my fuel tank with alternate servings of beer and ice cream.

The town of Quincy is nestled in a laid-back, rural environment. It sports an untamed lifestyle to which I aspire. It is a place of contentment and stability, volunteer firefighters and gazebos, barbershops and courthouses, county fairs and country stores, parades and evening strolls. The people here share wholesome values, common purpose, and unpretentiousness.

Belden Bliss

Day 67 - July 13. My internal engine cranks and Jerry paces me north to tiny Belden. It is a supreme treat to have a compatible shadow. For only the second time this summer, part of my gear is shared. This permits me free reign along the hellish three dozen or so switchbacks that eventually drop down to the North Fork of the Feather River. Moving almost effortlessly without the tug of freight, I feel like a spirited colt.

We dance along this wandering treadmill, gobbling up the distance as a duo. The surface is in great shape through recently christened Bucks Lake Wilderness. Our journey climaxes with a vigorously executed, blissful dip in the river. A friendly wind whistles through fine sandbar striations.

Some years back a three-day storm literally destroyed the Belden Lodge and surrounding campgrounds, but spared the general store. The latter houses a closet-sized cafe and stumpy counter stools. The post office, 75 yards to the west, would fit in your bathroom.

Thirty-one is a lot of miles   Janis Mumford

Day 68 - July 14. Following a daybreak coffee fix, I walk over to that
rustic post office where a gabby country clerk grins through several
randomly distributed teeth. She brushes an accumulation of dust off a
battered trail box that has been waiting to be claimed. I had arranged for
it to be mailed what now seems like ages ago.

After eating several goodies that would crowd my pack, I cross many
intersecting rivulets along Chips Creek while making my way toward the
sweeping meadows bordering Cold Springs.

The skittish, busy work of chipmunks, the warm scent of pine, and
multi-colored flower gardens dominate the morning scene. A daredevilish
hawk's cry is sucked up into the air current and echoes off to nowhere.
Four deer line my path and stare at me through the brush. Dust and sweat
coagulate into sun-caked mud on my furrowed brow. I arch my shoulders
back to offset a rounded posture as a pesky liquid film of perspiration drips
from my face like tears.

Featherly airborne robbers, gray and greedy, keep watch on my progress, playing tag from limb to limb. I am a brash stranger in a highland
of tiny cupped ponds, pinnacles with teeth, and 50-mile views across
unpeopled acreage.

I drink an extra quart of liquid at lunch as a toast to the growing
distance between me and my starting point. I feel strongly that I will
complete this journey.

I run the downhills conservatively, thereby placing special emphasis
on the day's critical second half. This keeps my energy level up. With my
running already hindered by the instability of my pack, this also prevents
me from overextending myself into catatonic stumbling.

Tonight's bivouac area is fenced in to keep out the cattle population. I spend time filing down calluses and softening the blemished exteriors of both feet. Fortunately, the pus splotches and itching from the poison oak have subsided. Stifling a chuckle, I vow aloud never to nimwittingly lay the hip belt in the wrong bushes.

I look skyward to find the rising moon which begins to bathe the trail in a tint of rubbed silver.

By now I have developed a keen awareness of all trail forks, signed or otherwise. I often find myself needing an extra time cushion where a demoralizing unmarked maze or mental mistake might trigger a wrong turn. Updated Forest Service maps that show newly reconstructed side trails lend added security should I need an emergency escape route. Occasional mileage markers are illegible or incorrect due to gradation improvements lengthening the distance. Some have misspelled words. Accurate forward progress is earned by mapwork, guesswork, and prayer.

On this survival shuffle through the uncertain and the unknown, I rememorize every side trail and stream crossing prior to each day's run.

The trail is usually better cared for in Northern California than in its southern counterpart. In many instances, marker emblems are carefully engraved with a black woodburned imprint on a varnished brown background.

There is a noticeable difference in impact between rock-hard fire roads and soft dirt trails. On rest days I notice the jarring lack of resiliency in concrete, as well as asphalt that has not been recently surfaced.

On rainy days I look back in appreciation to the luxury of fast-drying brown dirt where a narrow canyon or north-facing ridgeline doesn't block out the sun. Wet, black-hued dirt in shaded areas can be a virtual quagmire and potential ankle wrencher, especially in the late afternoon when fatigue is inevitable.

One only need visualize the number of required footplants to appreciate the odds of a possible fall. A major mishap here will ruin five years of planning. I am too determined. Failure to cautiously prepare and execute is preparing to fail.

Day 69 - July 15. Today's 30-miler, 23 of it waterless, tracks me over Humboldt Summit to Highway 36. After nine hours of solitude, while running inconspicuously over the shale ledge that overlooks Lake Almanor, I barrel into 15 Boy Scouts repairing a bridge at Soldier Creek. This is only the second time I have encountered anyone on the trail since Donner Pass, two weeks ago. They stare in a befuddled stupor at my primeval wardrobe.

I share a toast in this secluded setting, then span their nearly completed handiwork. We wish each other well and I bound toward the sounds and smells of another town.

As a human steward networking with nature and attempting to make sense out of life, I find that I am no longer the person who began this adventure. Each new day has added substance and cohesion to my human spirit as a brand-new, unique trail section unfolds its glorious mysteries and surprise friendships.

I head into Chester where mounds of chicken and veggie stir-fry promise to hone the sharp corners of the day. A comforting, magic elixir brewed up by Lew and Joanna Knickerbocker — whom I met so many miles ago in the Southern Sierra — now becomes a reality.

As I enjoy this special evening, I wonder who else I will meet along the way. I recognize this need for balance, peopled evenings and singular nights side by side. I am not yet sure how I'll incorporate it into the "real world." Perhaps I will find some way to continue this journey on a smaller basis, and that will suffice. The thought is a difficult one, and lest I let it spoil this night, I make an effort to banish it and live in the moment.

Taking it all in from a hard earned vantage point   by Lee Freeman

6 Levitating Through Lassen _____

By thine own soul learn to live,
And if men thwart thee, take no heed,
If men hate thee, have no care;
Sing thou thy song, and do thy deed, hope thou thy hope
and pray thy prayer.

— Parkenham Beatty

Bubble Pots and Channel 7

Day 70 - July 16.   A contemplative respite in Chester.

Day 71 - July 17.   Today, after a reindoctrination into civilization, I gently amble to Terminal Geyser, Drakesbad Ranch, and Warner Camp. I stop at Little Willow Lake to sign the Pacific Crest Trail register which is kept dry within a huge metal box. This spot in Lassen Park is roughly halfway between Mexico and Canada. It also used to be a notorious giardia area until the beaver were removed.

The odor of sulphur from surrounding calderas and fumaroles wells up in my nostrils as I run through this alpine pressure cooker. Several knee-deep swamps bottom out with foot-thick muck and goo, like small traps within a cradling, jungle-like forest. I imagine that right now I appear to the world around me as a half-naked animated speck slogging through this primeval land of volcanic remnants.

Drakesbad's century-old resort offers tranquility and a sense of place amidst geyser-laden fire and brimstone. A web of soothing, gurgling streams meander through this high-mountain playground. A deeply hued sky bathes a vivid landscape that blends rich pine aromas, tempered only by the froth of mildly sulfuric water and steam. I briefly leave the main path to visit Devil's Kitchen, a conglomerate of mudpots sequestered on the fringe of a shoehorn-shaped canyon.

Lassen uses some metal signs, far more durable than wood. Many Pacific Crest Trail diamond markers are red, instead of silver, within the National Park. This is a welcome treat in contrast to the unmarked terrain a short while ago.

I am intrigued upon witnessing several wild turkeys and grouse rigorously competing for pecking order near two marshy ponds. The setting sun shoots spears of amber light through a realm of trees. A bevy of smaller birds explodes into flight with thunderous wing flapping, temporarily interrupting my reverie.

Evening stretching has become more than a ritual. It is now mandatory as a means of allowing the muscles to return to their former suppleness.

Loosening up at trailhead near Chester   Lew Knickerbocker

After meditating on constantly changing images within the pulsating
fireside coals, I serenade the woodlands with some melodious snoring. I
awaken once to witness two taut lower limbs quivering uncontrollably.
Looking skyward, I follow the pathway of a falling star as it streaks across
the spectrum of galaxies and constellations.

Day 72 - July 18. Daylight launches me on another grueling exploit
with stops at Feather, Silver, and Cluster lakes. A muscle-soothing swim
across the latter reinforces my determination, and I remember why I came.

Silence is interrupted as a large-billed swan skitters over the lake on
its huge feet and lunges awkwardly into the air. Several rising trout dimple
the surface with intermittent jumps. A small doe carcass lies half buried
behind a hollowed-out blade of driftwood, the putrid remains covered with
clusters of buzzing flies. Her spine is brutally snapped, her jaw frozen
shut. The gore sends my stomach churning. For a moment, it seems
incomprehensible that such violence can coexist with the peace and natural

beauty of this place. In embracing nature, we are forced to accept the reality of its "flip side," but at times I wish I could ignore it.

A slippery log-crossing tests my balance but precludes a deep river ford near the lake outlet. I am a little shaky. Having to be "on" so much of the time jeopardizes my patience level. I feel fortunate that I scheduled my rest days the way I did; I didn't realize back then how much I'd need them.

Days 73-74 - July 19-20.   Heading down to "Old Station" under Mt. Lassen's protective guardianship, I'm bundled off by Lew and Joanna Knickerbocker for some effective rejuvenation in tiny Shingletown, site of their cottage in the pines. It seems so long ago that we met. I am heartily impressed by the way they followed through with their offer of lodging and honored that they treat me like a longtime friend — not a trailside acquaintance.

The following day Channel 7 in Redding highlights my passage through this pristine domain in a ten-minute news blurb. The reporters interviewing me are interested in the pioneer adventure aspect, my minimal garb, and my mind's constant battle in recovering from successive 12-hour days.

Ah! The Wilderness!

Day 75 - July 21.   Following heavenly rest in a real bed, one of the finest marathon showers ever, and several natural food meals, I return to the trail for a 25-miler to primitive Cassel. The footing is poor along the granulated, monotonous escarpment, but the sensitizing wonders of Lassen Volcanic National Park streamline the effort.

Today's itinerary offers varied blockbusting ingredients: sharp briars, a four-wheeler-rutted road, no water, indiscriminately logged areas, and ball bearing-like pumice that kneads my feet for miles of stride lengths. The rye-like grass attracts hordes of tiny mice, making it a notorious rattler den.

Massive sections of hot, jagged lava cut at my tender foot bottoms like cruel, primitive shaping tools. My running shoes stick to the overheated surface — lava is clearly a poor heat conductor. Ridge silhouettes vault into the clouds and spiky trees penetrate a graying sky. I feel as if I am traversing a bleak, eerie ribbon of the moon. Sturdy old timber straggles over high ridges and hangs on as if to defy the sheer cliffs.

It is almost as if I am watching an animated film when I look around me. Crafty squirrels strip the huge cones from stunted pines which land on the ground with the force of small grenades. The forest comes alive with birds swooping down from the sky. A tiny water bug draws a thread of light within the minuscule whirlpool of an algae-filled pond. A yucca puffball drifts across the water and rises again, too light to be trapped by the surface tension.

The wind blows up at my feet, flattening the grass, bending the trees, then whipping my face with dust and brown pine needles. A black-bellied thundercloud bears up the valley toward me.

My back begins to creak and my hips ache. Nonetheless, I am alone in a bowl of peaks and delighted to be here.

Day 76 - July 22. I jaunt over to nearby Burney for a nurturing package and some hot pasta in a friendly cafe. It seems to be inhabited by half the town. Following a live radio interview, I sleep on the office floor rug of a church as there are no campgrounds.

Day 77 - July 23. A special Sunday dawn tribute has me briefing the congregation about the solo, unencumbered aspect of the run. I then run north over well-denuded private land near Crystal and Baum lakes. Roily clouds bring moisture-laden, impenetrable gloom. I end up getting bathed in stages.

Tonight's wet camp at Burney Falls State Park is near a main road and store. My portable home lies under a hastily constructed lean-to.

Day 78 - July 24. First light initiates a rugged 30-mile stretch between Lake Brittain and Moosehead Springs. The sun fans its warmth across the terrain in impatient golden spokes, transposing a somber cloud bank into silhouettes.

The ensuing climbs are tough and hard earned. My lungs heave with the effort. Raw beauty and open freedom are everywhere. Invigorating creekside melodies serenade my push on.

I think about the contrast between this regenerative refuge I've entered and the mechanized world now behind me. I try to drink in a sense of time and place that these mountains unpretentiously offer. I feel excited and alive. I am one darn fortunate human being.

I bivouac in a ravine and build a small fire to foster a warm spirit. Shadows dance 100 feet tall against a rock face. Nearby crystalline pools lie individually cupped in stone. The pulsating evening tints paint the landscape with emotion and a cleansing sincerity.

I reflect, motivated that everyone I meet has been so heartening. I'd be climbing at altitude with a fanny pack, running shorts, white hat, no shirt, and run right into a group of flabbergasted hikers with gargantuan packs. They would predictably query me about my destination and inevitably a detailed conversation ensues. We all need to get out into the woods to rediscover the pleasures of spontaneous interaction.

I am getting earlier starts here than in the higher Southern Sierra. Those nights were much damper. All my cloth items had to be dried out for an hour in the rising sun before I could roll, band, zip, and run. It has taken substantial practice to get the pack to a point where shifting is minimal. Sometimes I place a rolled up polypro sweatshirt just below my lower back to simulate a wedge.

Meticulous hydration is essential on cold days as well. It is important not to wait until thirst encourages you to drink since thirst is not a good liquid-need criteria.

Dehydration can occur 50% faster above 9,000 feet than at sea level. To compensate for the reduced oxygen content of the air and reduced cardiac output, you breath deeper and more rapidly. But the air is dryer at altitude and this spurs dehydration. Therefore, one needs to increase fluid intake at these altitudes and subsequently you urinate more.

I suppose most people learn this critical information eventually. Too often a novice learns it too late after suffering an incident resulting from poor planning. Being underinformed can be tragic. Although rare, athletes do die in sporting events simply because they didn't prepare their bodies adequately, or worse, because they falsely believed their bodies were invincible. When I read these things, I always feel this terrible mixture of sadness and frustration. In my coaching I make a point of getting the information across no matter how much the individual resists.

Day 79 - July 25. I rise upon spotting a skittish fox and contemplate the day's marathon across the forested solitudes below Grizzly Peak.

The steep, grueling push around a decimated ridgeline equals Idyllwild's Desert Divide ascent in energy expenditure. God's bold handicraft dominates each furlong. I wave to the person manning the Grizzly Peak fire lookout 500 feet above me, then move on toward Deer Creek and Ash Camp. A good-sized thunderhead dumps its sizable contents and I become a sodden but briskly moving trash bag.

Much of the Pacific Crest Trail is built on the south and west slopes in order to avoid the less sunny areas where snow lingers. The frustrating side-slope of the trail, usually on my left side, breaks down my running shoes faster than flat terrain. I also unconsciously lean outward from the mountain for hours.

This third day after a layover is predictably tough. I am less limber and my freight feels heavier than its actual weight. By afternoon I am kicking rocks, roots, and my own ankles.

A coyote now crosses my path. Farther along, in an overgrown quagmire, rattlers are frequent and I confront three within 15 minutes.

A rickety pickup truck starts to pass me on a nearby, parallel dirt road and then stops. The heavily bearded, white-haired, male driver shuttles me 18 miles to the quaint railroad town of McCloud where I tenderize some slightly frozen human tissue. The rain is coming down in buckets when I stagger in, a total stranger. God's grace being what it is, this changes quickly. Resident Chips Thompson, who saw the Redding telecast, recognizes me and offers to house my shriveled remains under his roof. I heave an audible sigh of relief as I watch him toss all of my clammy gear into his dryer.

Days 80-81 - July 26-27.   While I am having breakfast the next morning the waitress volunteers to loan me her archaic bike to expedite my errands. I decline as the entire town is easily accessible on foot. The overwhelming effusiveness of this idyllic retreat is a carbon copy of Wrightwood and Idyllwild.

Traffic around the square is almost nonexistent. A muddied pickup sits next to a bathroom-sized school bus. This is the heart of history, a fondly restored railroad town steeped in American tradition — a Norman Rockwell painting come to life: country store, five-and-dime, and soda fountain. Friendly folks live here and bring up polite, well-scrubbed kids in a close knit setting within an envelope of rarified air. I can't help but believe that life is more meaningful here than in our urban, mechanized existence.

The farther north I go the more laid-back it is. There is a feeling of more freedom. There are fewer laws. You don't even need a watch. You don't have to pretend. People accept you the way you are.

It is an unselfish and cleaner world. People are more caring about their neighbors. They actually listen to what others have to say instead of constantly interrupting or impatiently waiting for an opening so they can talk.

It is Sunday and I feel a tinge of pride as an honored guest inside historic St. Joseph's Church. This rustic structure sports proud beams of chocolate brown and white geometric stripes.

Bob and Patti Carpenter whirl in from Southern California on a motorcycle. Their company highlights a warm and rewarding 48 hours. This is the same Bob Carpenter who hiked in a food cache (that included selective cervezas) to Bill McDermott and me in the High Sierra during my first summer on the trail.

I consider the circumstances. Only one day before I was monsooned off a mucky trail ribbon by numbing downpours that forced me down to lower elevation. Now I am honored by a series of impromptu mini-fests on village porches. At a marvelously entertaining square dance in the town hall tonight, I fantasize myself out there on the floor in borrowed duds. What a sharp contrast it would make to the meager "uniform" I have worn throughout this journey.

Skirting Shasta's Bold Outreaches

Day 82 - July 28.   At first light of a new day, Bob Carpenter shuttles me back to nature and its rebellious ways. I reconnect with a 27-miler over debilitating topography. I dodge three more rattlers on the badly angled grind along Girard Ridge en route to Castle Crags State Park near Castella. This segment earns a special award for blatant indifference to humans. Jungle-like vegetation on both sides rub green noses with regularity to make passage barely tolerable.

An exuberant Bob motors over to the park's hiker camp, then runs seven miles east to coax me along. Pacific Crest Trail hikers who pass

Lunch catered by caring support crew   by Lew Knickerbocker

through tiny Castella are usually privileged to meet Milt Kenney, retired logger and self-proclaimed "Mayor of the Pacific Crest Trail." He recently lost both his wife and sister, withstood open heart surgery, and now dedicates his life to shepherding PCT hikers. Whether it is a hot meal, shoe repair, trail updates, transportation to a larger town in his relic of a vehicle — whatever you might need — Milt cannot do enough. Most importantly, you are treated to his endless knowledge.

Milt intercepts us as we arrive at the park's trailhead. The date on my post office cache has clued him of our upcoming arrival. Within minutes we are hastened to nearby Dunsmuir as his dinner guests.

Browsing in Dunsmuir's "Old Town," we indulge to excess at an old-time soda fountain. At tonight's ranger-naturalist program in the local campground, I speak on the planning and endurance aspects of my journey. The camp's heavily wooded site is one of the finest facilities on or near the trail. The drone of moving metal on bordering Interstate 5 proves its only drawback.

Day 83 - July 29. Bob and Patti bid me adieu at dawn. A troublesome solo 32-mile day dishes out a thrashing up to a saddle well above the rugged crags. The climb is unyielding. This trail can break you if you outpace yourself. My hamstrings convulse during the inaugural 14 miles which are 90 percent uphill. This section includes punishing chunks of elevation gain that mandate clean, hard effort. I carefully monitor food and water intake to keep my energy level up. The ascent demands complete concentration. My eyes constantly jump between stumps, rocks, roots, hidden holes, and potential rattler confrontations.

The undulating turf overlooks Mumbo and Gumboot lakes. I run into a friendly, hardworking trail crew led by an efficient college woman. They are clearing brush a yard back on each side. Removing the thistles, thick stocks, and gnarly roots is slow, tedious business. This contingent clearly enjoys a seemingly insurmountable task. On rest breaks they share the solitude among exquisite panoramas. It is evident they take personal pride in manicuring this National Scenic Trail.

One hour later, a rousing good luck toast from a half-full ceramic mug proffered by a wandering camper helps soften the rigors of my struggle. I recognize the symptoms that follow these especially difficult days when I have to keep pulling from a reservoir already dangerously low. I sometimes fear I will wake up in the morning and be unable to move my limbs — that I'll just lie there looking upward until hunger and dehydration begin to suck the life out of me.

Is it helpful to think such thoughts or does it just damage the spirit? I am of two minds about it. On one hand, it seems an almost necessary exercise because it helps me find a contrast in emotion at the other end of the spectrum.

The other element is that depressive thoughts can be debilitating. When physical survival is almost entirely in my hands during this journey, the thought of emotional depletion wreaking havoc on my body is frightening.

That old cliche "tomorrow is another day" feels oddly comforting. For a moment I chuckle at finding solace in those battered words.

It is short lived, though. I am once again somber as I build a small fire, and without any thought for the taste of it, I down some dried food.

When sleep begins pulling me in feet first, I end this last waking hour with thoughts of an unscheduled siesta at upcoming Porcupine Lake. I wonder if it is foresight or intuition that has me planning more than my normal amount of rest at this juncture. Whatever the reason, I'm grateful.

Primitive Days and Nocturnal Surprises

Day 84 - July 30.   Early light kicks off a lackluster 29-mile odyssey to Scott Mountain Summit via Upper Deadfall, Bluff, and Bull lakes. Stunted trees, olive-hued peaks, and talus scars dot this colossal escarpment. Forward propulsion becomes somewhat laborious by late afternoon as my leg muscles begin to twinge and whimper.

I run the final moments in darkness. I sleep at the trail's edge on a benign, brown-needle carpet within a dense pine forest. Dark boughs encircle me like protective arms.

Around midnight a woman who has just quarreled with her boyfriend decides to walk on the trail. She is carrying her sleeping bag and a B.B. gun for protection. She steps on me with her full weight as I am sawing logs in my inconspicuous make-shift campground. She is laden with the grotesque stench of alcohol and nicotine, and has not had a bath for days.

I shine my tiny flashlight groggily upward and pinpoint two and a half teeth missing in the front. Her matted, shoulder-length hair presents an unnerving blend of unkempt and uncombed. A partially torn peasant gown drags wearily over the turf.

She mutters several unpleasantries about the argument, falls heavily to the ground, and then passes out in an audible stupor.

After a bracket of lonely days on the trail, one might dream of a surprise nocturnal companion. This is not her — I didn't want to breathe too deeply or touch anything. At dawn she will mutter a slurred adieu and stagger off to somewhere as I psych up for the day.

Day 85 - July 31. Following that sleepless night I run north throughout an uneventful morning. As I round a bend at midday, a sizeable middle-aged woman, shaped somewhat like a human fireplug, aims a video camera at my legs. When I pause to chat she exuberantly blurts out this

An uninvited guest   by Mike Dirham

one-liner: "I haven't seen any live game out here in quite a while." She calls herself a "meandering doddler" who has fallen well behind her coed hiking entourage of retired seniors. I find her conversation interestingly philosophical. She is trying to turn a sedentary life around with effort and attitude. She is motivated by what I am doing and not startled by my sudden, scantily-clad appearance. I praise her gritty spunk and move on.

I hitch a ride to tiny Callahan for a resupply cache. I shower, shave, and rest at a nearby ranger station. Outside, distant peaks disappear into twilight as colors drain from the sky.

Tonight coyotes sing songs to the moon under kaleidoscoped galaxies. The wind cries out in the crisp sub-alpine air that slices through my campsite. I resemble a monk, as self-sufficient as I can ever remember.

Day 86 - August 1. A local wilderness ranger returns me to the trail-head. A stellar 20-mile day pushes me through the northern tip of the Trinity Alps, by East Boulder Lake toward Carter Meadow, and on into the Marble Mountain Wilderness watershed. The area's passionate grandness stokes up an excited inner core. One ridgeline segment is in atrocious condition, but I complain to no one until I invest my own sweat in a volunteer trail-clearing effort.

I am becoming increasingly less enamored with my sense of self. This is no place for pomposity or unwarranted self-assuredness. Entertaining either could prove disastrous.

The sojourn to Etna Summit is accomplished with consummate ease along a refreshingly high quality corridor. The trail is literally blasted through granite, reminiscent of many similar overhanging ledges in the Sierra.

Three horse-size elk crash by like linebackers, hastily massaging my adrenalin. The big hulks lumber off authoritatively leaving me still trembling from their jackhammer-like passage. An invigorating swim across Paynes Lake calms my nerves and refreshes my spirit for the afternoon finale.

The sweetness of addictive salmonberries lubricate some bland tastebuds en route.

A trucker drives me down to the Scott Valley Drug Store in Etna. After gulping three hot sandwiches, each washed down with a distinctive imported cerveza, I prepare tonight's sleeping quarters. I select a bronze grass strip, buffered with a blanket of soft leaves, on the outskirts of town.

7 Quintessential Cascades _____

We need to praise running for what it is. There are safer ways to exercise than this, better ways to meditate, quicker ways to get high, truer ways to find religion, easier ways to have fun. I don't deny that running gives some of those things. But praising them too highly hides what we really have here — a sport, which like all sports, has both pain and joy, risk and reward.

— Joe Henderson

Trail Protocol #1

Day 87 - August 2. Today I enjoy a layover in Etna. A perseverance in weathering the elements and terrain every step of the way has made me a better person; that's all anyone can ask from life. On a run that is 90 percent mental I work daily on a positive attitude to cover any character flaws.

Once off the trail, we take each other for granted within our distraction-filled, clockwork existence. We need to develop a more simplistic awareness of natural things as our passage through this wonderful land is far too brief. We do not treasure human qualities and the enthralling splendor of nature nearly enough.

Good friends Rick and Donna Fay drive in from Auburn to hike my regular, newly supply-filled pack into the Marble Valley guard station. Tonight we provide each other with trail updates while sharing a delicious meal. I'm concerned about a reputed snow patch above Cliff Lake that can be steep, icy, and harrowing.

Day 88 - August 3. Fortunately, that dreaded snow patch proves passable when I traverse its crest this morning. I am alone on this 29-miler, moving on crusty granules along a glacial plateau. The path has completely dropped away at three precarious spots.

I regress in dreamy visualization of supine sunbathing on a South Pacific island while sipping nectar. However, today's compensating blessing is being able to get through this chaos with less supplies sandwiched inside my pack. In it are the barest of survival essentials: dried food, polypropylene layers, matches, topo maps, fire starter paste, a whistle, space blanket, iodine tabs, a tiny flashlight, compass, trash bag raincoat, snake bite kit, ankle brace, PowerBars, and Bodyfuel. I hand carry all my liquid.

I visit with stretched out hikers in Shelly Meadow. Later a tingling plunge into Marten Lake brightens the day.

As I continue north on the trail, a huge black bear crashes into the scene, momentarily shattering my easy-going tempo. He pauses a split

Man versus beast   by Mike Dirham

second just off the trail, standing high at the shoulders, with powerful forelegs and cat-like hooked claws. His burly head and husky jaw muscles shoot the hair on my back and neck straight up. I take several deep breaths to slow the staccato-like beating of my adrenalin-charged heart.

I stand my ground, realizing that since this is the middle of the summer the bear's chief staple is wild fruit (especially berries), and as such, he'd have no appetite for human flesh. Also, no cubs are in sight. The ground shakes for a few seconds with his exiting sprint which all but obliterates a side ravine's stunted growth.

Bears are poorly sighted creatures that often have difficulty pinpointing stationary figures in a background setting. However, their audible faculties are outstanding and their sense of smell is unmatched in the wild. For dessert, a bear's ill-mannered feeding ritual might include shredding off large scab-like slabs of outer tree bark, sometimes several yards high. This creates a tantalizing haven for insects and opportunistic birds that eat them.

During the day's final hour, a copious flower garden mellows me. Wild bouquets and intoxicating scents abound. It is so lush that the delicate petals hit my face as well as brushing my body.

Alongside the path, rivulets seep through tiny channels in the solid rock; a common sight around Marble Mountain.

As my trip progresses I find myself pushing harder on the days I feel especially good, then shortening the next one or breaking it up with extra rest stops. I can only make these alterations when I don't have a pre-planned meeting with a support person.

On the respites, I'll often lie in the warm, gentle grass and let the sun restore me, then stare tirelessly at the mountains. The oncoming dusk invariably rewards me with its pink hues on west-facing vertical walls.

Still of major concern is drinking water quality. A decade ago, cold, clear moving water in this area could have been completely trusted, but bacterial contamination has become a significant issue today. The potential for ingesting the bacteria is one I can't risk since the aftereffects might necessitate my aborting the rest of the trip.

A careless camper has polluted the Paradise Lake outlet with detergent and trout innards, an ultimate breach of wilderness etiquette. A baby fawn diffuses my anger as it ambles over to share my lakeside site while I gather wood. It huddles and stares before finally darting off.

Day 89 - August 4. Despite constant care, toe and heel blisters continue to crop up and are excruciatingly painful. Caused invariably by the combination of pack weight and poor surface, the condition is exacerbated by the friction resulting from my foot's inevitable swelling as daily mileage accumulates. In addition, my protective insert pads sometimes get dislodged and scrunch my toes together. This causes a hammertoe effect and intense localized throbbing. Even when I allow a clear gap between the big toe and shoe front, along with ample width, problems can and do still occur.

My discipline and patience are both at stake. I ice these sore areas in the coldest stream I can find and psyche up for my upcoming encounter with Jan Levet who has checked trail registers and expects me today.

Jan, one of the top female runners in the United States and holder of many trail race records, drives for six hours to sheep-dung contaminated Grider Creek. She will later run a stretch of the trail with me, but tonight is armed to the teeth with goodies. For openers there's "Dagwood" sandwiches, ice cold beer, fresh shoes, and a crushing hug. She's a true friend and, as one of the first women ever to hike the Pacific Crest Trail solo, she is someone with whom I have a special connection. We have lots of bear-confrontation and baby-fawn-born-on-the-trail stories to share. Jan Levet pens her feelings on why we come to the trail:

> "I often reflect on spiritual accomplishments. Putting up with the long days and miles; buckets of sweat; falls and bruises; and hours of scratchy poison oak, truly requires unshakable self-discipline, developed over years of physical and mental training in facing the unpredictable.
>
> High, hilly mountain trails have allowed me to reach for a simplicity and serenity within myself which no other person has ever given me. I can look further inward for a sense of exploration, discovery and satisfaction that no societally-fabricated job has ever given me, nor ever will.
>
> My journeys along mountain paths have given me openness, freedom, and limitless space. Long runs take me away from the confines of walls and Sunflex miniblinds, away from work-related administrivia — a crashing breakaway from the envelope of comfort and luxury in which we so frequently find ourselves. With running I can stretch myself, take risks, or at least be uncertain of the outcome of heading down that open road. I prefer to disdain life's artificial limitations, and challenge myself, remaining solidly committed to forging my own rules on my own life."

Day 90 - August 5. Jan shuttles some gear and I run solo the short distance from Grider Creek to Seiad Valley. Although the logistics were prearranged, it seems that fellow wilderness runner Lee Freeman appears out of nowhere later that afternoon. The booming thunderclaps, crackling lightning, and torrential rain have drenched and turned him ashen.

Combining his own personal adventure with mountain sherpa assistance for me, Lee throttled his aging vehicle over 30 miles of Forest Service fire roads to a God-forsaken cow swamp called "Alex Hole." He then ran 28 miles south on the Pacific Crest Trail to Seiad Valley where he will pace me the exact distance back. He will perform a similar service a week later in Oregon on a 23-miler between Siskiyou Summit and Hyatt Lake. Lee is one of the toughest minded, hardest working, and most positive thinking trail masochists I know. He is the epitome of selflessness.

A friendly chance meeting with Chris Hawk, owner (at this writing) of Hawk's Roost Resort in picturesque Seiad Valley, my final California supply depot, averts a wet-weather bivouac. She provides the three of us with lodging (a rug on the floor of her rumpus room for a nominal $2).

Rest day at Seiad Valley   by Chris Hawk

Day 91 - August 6. In the morning Chris introduces us to the entire town, later has dinner with us in the local cafe, and bakes us goodies for the journey. Tomorrow, as an encore, she will cheerlead us back to the mud-slaked trailhead when it is time to move on.

Other than a seven-mile stretch east of Castle Crags, I've been solo since Jerry Blinn ran into Belden Camp with me a month ago. This is day 33 since leaving Donner Pass. I welcome with anticipation the upcoming presence of dual pacers.

A constant source of humor evolves from human encounters. Backpackers inquisitively study me as if I have just arrived from another planet. During long lonely stretches I would meet up with these active, congenial hikers just when I needed their motivating encouragement the most. They are a refreshing change from the often harried and complaining urbanite. It's hard to go unnoticed in the wild where genuine camaraderie comes easily. I have come to cherish my temporary stint as a self-styled drifter with a well-defined goal.

Some of us vastly underestimate the mountains. They're not dangerous, they're just indifferent. With so much time on the trail you learn to analyze overbearing situations and make good, careful judgments. An ornery, yet safety-oriented, stubbornness accompanies each chunk of progress.

Day 92 - August 7. Following the exhilarating rest at Seiad Valley, I now share the trail with personable Jan and indestructible Lee.

We survive the threat of possible trail closure because of numerous lightning-ignited fires still burning. A parade of colorful parachutes, left by smoke jumpers, decorate the pathway as we ramble north. We are tempted to open the alluring food packages dropped for the firefighters, but opt for photos instead. In these situations, the first jumpers fan out to contain the flames, and a second crew comes in later to mop up.

After a midday lunch stop amongst mesmerizing vistas, it is time for Jan to exchange warm hugs and head back down the trail to civilization.

An ever upward 12-hour day finds Lee and I pouncing with iron nerves over Devil's Peak, Red Butte, and Cook and Green passes. We are forced to swill from some stagnant, intimidating watering holes. Upon hobbling into Alex Hole we experience anger at twenty cows standing in the only liquid available — a small spring-fed pond. Nearby waits Lee's old car where he parked it two days before.

Lee breaks out two folding cots, cold sandwiches, and a couple of warm beers from his mud-caked vehicle. We are soon primed for motionless slumber under a star-studded canopy.

California Collared

Day 93 - August 8. I rise when it's light enough to see, repack my fanny pack, and dispense my hugs of appreciation and adieu to Lee Freeman.

It is a source of amazement to me and to others that Lee has offered to go to great lengths to meet me in each of the three states. It's well beyond the call of duty, even for such a close friend. And it isn't as if he travels in style, either. He will be drive these thousands of miles in an old beat-up Volkswagen Bug that he clearly cherishes. Then, after the road rattle, he punishes himself on some of the most difficult parts of the trail.

Lee explains that his reasons for doing this, in the greater scheme of things, are really quite simple:

> "It's an elemental thing, which really gets down to the fact that we'll 'never pass this way again' and I wanted to be there.
>
> Bob leaned on me a little, saying he wanted me to be here, but that wasn't the reason I came. I knew I had a great deal to learn just being with him. He knows these trails like the back of his hand, which I think is incredible — he actually even knows the location of each watering hole. When you consider it, it's a very different system of landmarks, and infinitely more romantic than the street signs and buildings we rely upon here to find our direction.
>
> I went for the adventure, which is a sure thing when you're with Bob. When he was planning the trip, Bob sent around a support-team list to about 35 of us. It was more like a calling than a request, as far as I'm concerned. And we all know what we miss if we ignore a calling. Somehow, I just knew I'd be there.
>
> What's ironic is that Bob fits the perfect mold of the coach; he's highly disciplined and regimented, and ultimately opinionated. For instance, his face reddens at the merest mention of the big-time ball players and their outrageous salaries — he sees and feels the injustice in it. The people who actually put these athletes on the map are paid such low wages and rarely get any recognition at all. It's a valid grievance. I can only assume he did what he did in his career for the love of it.
>
> When my friends found out what I was doing, they thought I was crazy — 'all that driving for what?' they asked.
>
> My answer is simple: I have an appointment."

After hunkering down the trail for a couple of hours, I head into Oregon. I celebrate by munching a granola bar next to a tiny border sign tacked on a tree. Running has become my daily, self-inflicted, wilderness assignment. I wonder whether I still know how to drive.

The trail is strewn with cattle dung. Grazing is permitted on Forest Service land for a fee, but to hikers' dismay, "pooper scooper" legislation has not yet reached the high country. I momentarily ignore these unsightly distractions to reflect upon more refreshing feelings.

It is a neat statement on life when my material world consists of one carry-on-the-hip pack.

Lightning fires clean the earth for fresh growth and the same is happening to me. Each day offers a brand new learning experience. Owning a myriad of superficial toys is not the key to happiness. Regardless of their image or value, they are still only transitory things.

The age and personality of rugged mountain trails has straightened out my priorities. This clarity of purpose instills a therapeutic tonic into my parched soul as I bed down under a sheltering secret place.

Day 94 - August 9.   Agonizing stretches after Wrangle Gap offer long hours of poorly signed footage with minimal water. I head for Siskiyou Summit and an ensuing Youth Hostel stopover in the congenial community of Ashland.

Both of my Velcro bottleholder straps have ripped apart and I will try to replace them tomorrow in town. This is my 94th day since leaving the Mexican border.

Tonight I hardly remember how to act, reuniting with life on a bunk bed mattress after watching a Shakespearean play. I relish my momentary escape from the smattering of crinkled leaves that line rock-littered trail tread.

Days 95-96 - August 10-11.   I sit alone in a small church shortly after dawn. Spiritual nourishment and deep gratitude dominate the morning. I have covered 1,640 miles of difficult, often badly cambered trail without major mishap. I hope I've eliminated all judgmental cockiness by now. I might experience anxiety, suffering, elation, loneliness, struggle, pleasure, sadness, and a desire to celebrate earned effort; all in the same day.

Whenever I pause to look south in a meditative moment, I visualize that Mexican boundary fence in its distant desert setting. It seems only yesterday that I stood beside it, stretching the kinks out. A dreamy intoxication and compelling imagination allow me to bare my cares to the mountain. I exult in this primeval life.

I rhythmically mesh with the environment while running free like the animals. My whole being almost ceases to exist. This incredible intimacy stems from total acceptance into that interconnected world of living things. I am at absolute peace within exhilarating exhaustion as I test myself in a different way. Any seemingly insurmountable obstacle in real society appears microscopic by comparison. I even feel the reverent touch of a Higher Power on truly tough days.

I have always believed in clean, rigorous outdoor activity. It encourages quality of life, good self-image, and an unabashed enthusiasm toward others. It is hard for me to explain this.

Wilderness running involves a few intimidating discomforts, but this sport has carved its way into my soul as I became enveloped by its sensual and emotional aspects.

A special spirit of adventure exists in all of us, but few have both the boldness and the opportunity to express it. We procrastinate our way through waking hours with tunnel vision, telling others what we'd like to do. But most of us never really instigate any kind of first step. I have tried to be a self-starter, stretching my own human potential by clean, honest exertion.

Next morning, the Ashland newspaper interviews me. I am so motivated that I bolt up a steep fire road toward nearby Mt. Ashland and this is a replenishment day. This accepting town ranks fondly in my mind with the three friendly places touted earlier. It also has some unsurpassed natural food restaurants. Feeling much the tranquil connoisseur, I will make a special effort to return.

Day 97 - August 12. A resourceful Lee Freeman rejoins me as we ascend toward limpid Hyatt Lake. The trail is in cracking good shape for it has recently been given an immaculate tailoring. We are in hog heaven upon finding three piped water sources along the trail.

Three black bear cubs are masticating huckleberries right on the path as we hustle around a bend at optimum speed. We send them scurrying up a rugged, barked pine.

The bear cubs play tree tag and perform reckless daredevil stunts. One trio member plummets off a low branch. It plops unharmed with an acrobatic two-point landing followed by a shoulder roll on soft duff. The cub bounces and frolics in the brush like a tiny professional tumbler giving a graceful, side stage performance. Another cub chews off the small limb supporting it and tumbles like a kitten to a lower support. And so it goes in this animal circus. Obviously, their mother was temporarily out scrounging for additional food. We quickly and quietly slip onward and do not challenge her return.

Any time one interacts with wildlife, one immediately drinks in all its associated anxiety. We are overly alert as we meander on toward Hyatt Lake Resort's more predictable environs.

Lee and I take a skinny dip, submerging all but our nose tips and a few goose bumps. Now we are hungry for the resort's "all you can eat" spaghetti dinner. A pair of ravenous warriors, we might have broken some kind of food consumption record. As a scarlet sunset wanes into the evening shadows, we feel eternally grateful for safe passage.

Day 98 - August 13. I reload the fanny pack in the morning, offer Lee an appreciative clasp of kinship, and I strike off alone to Lake of the Woods.

I pause only for a brisk swim across a mirrored, fresh water master-piece named Howard Prairie. A smattering of animal outcries announce my entry. Little chatterboxes from the squirrel kingdom sit high in the treetops broadcasting my whereabouts. These intelligent timber creatures seem to have specific words of alarm, distinguishable in tempo and length depending on the danger source.

A bear or human could draw an outburst of ear-piercing excitability as these animated, tufted furballs race up tree trunks. The sudden appear-ance of a hawk, lynx, or coyote might set off a series of automatic signals or an upward movement of collective voices. I personally receive many melodious calls in this well-guarded, living forest that stretches skyward.

I stagger into the resort at Lake of the Woods at twilight. The balls of my feet are raw and swollen, aggravated by a trail that has hardened from lack of moisture. The water at Lake of the Woods is too warm to reduce the swelling. There are no colder spring-fed creeklets in the immediate area. I am finally able to ease the pulsating soreness with ice from the resort store.

I study my topo maps while elevating rubbery lower limbs. Several of my toenails look like dog meat — blitzed from impact stress.

I copy a poem for an Oregon couple to impart to their handicapped son who is training for his premiere marathon. It is written by world famous blind athlete Harry Cordellos:

> *With faith that's strong,*
> *Your greatest goals*
> *You'll conquer bye and bye.*
> *Though disappointment threatens now,*
> *Don't be afraid to try.*
> *It really doesn't matter if you fail or drop the ball,*
> *The only real losers quit or never try at all .*
> *So give it everything you've got,*
> *And keep that courage high.*
> *If you do you'll win the prize*
> *That money cannot buy.*
> *You'll always walk with honor*
> *As there is no greater pride,*
> *Than knowing whether you win or lose*
> *With all your heart you tried.*

8 Oregon's Finest _____

Pain is inevitable, suffering is optional.

— Anonymous

Mosquito Madness

Day 99 - August 14.   A peaceful, rejuvenating rest day at Lake of the Woods.

Day 100 - August 15.   I reach the Rye Spur Trailhead as two huge trumpeter swans blast their eye popping early morning call. My 27-mile run through Sky Lakes Basin is highlighted by a tastebud pause at beautiful Isherwood Lake.

Mosquitos attack in squadrons, lapping up repellents. Outnumbered 100,000 to 1, I set a handslap record for dead and injured insects, but angry survivor pilots divebomb my eyeballs. Others use my lower lids for springboard assaults, bouncing back and forth between my sweat-laden face and the inner surface of my glasses. These marathon blitzes continue for several hours.

In the worst sections, I keep moving, cover all extremities, pull my hat down, collar up, and utilize the sideguards on my sunglasses. Even then a few stragglers manage to strain through my teeth. Only after I run up out of this mass breeding ground can I totally relax.

Trapper and Margurette lakes, two incandescent pearls, shimmer under late afternoon shafts of light. At Snow Lakes I take the Pacific Crest Trail alternate which veers up out of the basin. Tiny western frogs wander onto my path and energetic chickadees punctuate the croaking with their own song.

An hour later I playfully glissade over a short stretch of crusty snow that blankets the Pacific Crest Trail's main artery. Several impressive buttresses of ice-smeared volcanic rock dominate the setting.

I amble down to Cliff Lake to build a small fire, eat a light bite, rejoice, and then rest prostrate under a radiant sky.

Feeding Frenzy and Crater Lake

Day 101 - August 16.   Shortly after a brilliant dawn, a prominently antlered buck reacts to my invasion of his territory. He spurts off into some large conifers, then turns to stand staunchly, bellowing like a lunatic. He is immediately answered by one of Clark's nutcrackers, those audacious showman-like woodpeckers, wedging a pine nut into the bark of a tree.

An early morning departure   Robert Frickel

Woodpeckers continually cache precious nutrients into swiss cheese-like holes that they have drilled with staccato-sounding precision. In addition, they feed on the larva and adult forms of many harmful insects. The larger excavated cavities provide secondary housing for small owls, jays, and chipmunks.

Hikers love the trail much more in Oregon than in California. One patch looks like it was just manicured yesterday with even the rake marks still visible. Many side arteries lead to water or excellent camps in excellent repair. Untouched, a trail will deteriorate in three years and become unusable in five. I am soundly impressed by the tender loving care given to Oregon trails by the state's proud residents.

Midmorning I bump into a trio of Pacific Crest Trail hikers at Honeymoon Creek, earlier having learned of their presence from southbound travelers. We are buoyed by a simple meal and stirring tales.

After a nomadic cruise on fairly level terrain, I saunter into civilization at roadside Mazama Campground. As I return from a shower, Jim and Tina King — my Squaw Valley support duo — drive in from a triathlon to share a parcel of ground for the evening. This is a complete surprise.

Days 102-104 - August 17-19.   A reflective three-day respite at Crater Lake.

I have come to appreciate small things, like the indescribable joy of entering a tiny village grocery store and going wild on berries, cherries, and Haagen Dazs. After the tenth consecutive cold gorp snack, I visualize myself in front of a chicken burrito or large platter of fettucini alfredo, washing it down with a couple of exotic cervezas pulled from metal tubs of crushed ice.

At the post office I find a "go for it" note from Robert Freirich, Crater Lake marathon race director, tucked into a fruitful stash provided courtesy of Jan Levet. My excitement builds when I realize I'm just a half hour from magnificent Crater Lake. America's deepest, this icy, 1,932-foot deep jewel ranks as the world's seventh deepest lake. The lake is a study in color; the higher your vantage point, the deeper the hues are reflected.

The lake was created around 4000 B.C. by the self-destruction of Mt. Mazama whose powerful volcanic eruption was 36 times more powerful than the 1980 decapitation of Mount St. Helens. The eruption buried the landscape for 250 miles in every direction. Formerly the size of Mt. Hood, Mt. Mazama was replaced by a much smaller volcano known today as Wizard Island. I stare and wonder what it must have been like here before the eruption. Having heard of the area's effect on people who stay long enough to truly sense it, I decide to add extra rest days to bask in its aura.

From the rim above Crater Lake, rocky summits, perfectly outlined in the sharp, clear air, stretch in every direction. The tallest peaks catch the final rays of the sinking sun, burning with alpenglow. Beyond the twilight, a pastel sky is ribboned with apricot and baby blue. Somehow the fact that I have arrived here not by Winnebago, but via some 1,800 miles of footprints, makes the experience more enduring.

I share pizza and beer in the rim's Watchtower Lounge with the three hikers I met earlier on the trail. Such is our fatigue and the overwhelming beauty of this place that we find it difficult to make light conversation. We commune with very few words.

How different the world would be if each one of us followed a beckoning vision. One of the hikers, Oregon grocery chain owner Jim Girod, who had hooked up several weeks ago with veteran trekker Chuck Eidenschink and his girlfriend Dawn, has that same keen insight. He and I will cross paths again farther north, as he is walking the entire Pacific Crest Trail. Already he has lost 40 pounds and overcome the effects of 40 blisters. We became good friends on the spot when we met a few days earlier.

Day 105 - August 20. Alone again. Today I steer a rested frame northward. Scuds of pine duff and dust spin across the meandering trail. The forest creaks and moans under a cloud-dappled sky.

Two tall, rotting trees break off a few feet from their bottoms and plummet down, breaking my concentration. The violence of these natural acts is soon countered by the quiet satisfaction I feel when I reach a paved road after seven hours of running hidden in dense timber.

Upon arriving at Diamond Lake I am impressed by the friendliness and homespun tales of the storekeepers and cafe tenders. Local residents go out of their way to demonstrate a festive exuberance that somehow exceeds mere hospitality. I just hope I don't look too intimidating with my unshaven face, matted hair, and tattered uniform.

Before retiring, I scout out the next running day's trailhead. This research eliminates potential wrong-route frustrations. I simultaneously appraise the incoming cloud buildup, precursor to a possible storm.

Day 106 - August 21. Today a tumultuous rain washes the mountains and intensifies with alarming speed. Sleet coagulates into hailstones the size of marble agates. Lightning leapfrogs from cloud to cloud, cleaving the skies. A thunderbolt spirals down an isolated tree trunk. Strong winds drive the tranquil lake water into slapping, foaming waves.

This light show ignites over 40 fires in the area. Sheets of yellow flame lap at downed logs like unfurled flags flapping in the wind. This sucking inferno crackles in the trees as flames squirm up their main arteries. A horrendous roar literally dances down the slopes.

Fortunately, the fire stays above lake level. Several air tankers drop retardant on the larger trouble spots as well as those areas nearest to rural settlements. Most of the damage is not in the direction I am headed, but my apprehensions are honed. My tiny nocturnal campground lean-to shields out wetness but not the incessant noise of thunderclaps. Blistered bark and blackened stone create a naked, sterile wilderness.

Dad's Day

Day 107 - August 22. At dawn I gingerly slip away to quieter environs as smoke billows over hot spots. With a sweet gusto of abandon I head up Thielsen Creek, then skirt Maidu Lake on a 30-miler to Windigo Pass. Thick plumes of charcoal-colored haze enshroud both sun and moon for two days. Bleak stands of charred pines guard a burnt expanse. It wasn't as cataclysmic as an exploding mountain, but it convinced me of the land's restlessness.

A bevy of giddy squirrels pepper me with pine nuts along the way. Two lone elk bound by with authority as I reach the highpoint of the Pacific Crest Trail's northwest portion — 7,560 feet — just south of Tipsoo Peak's naked scree.

How fortunate I feel to find the path again in superb condition, flanked by hemlocks that mimic matchsticks.

Twenty miles is a walk in the park compared with successive 26 to 30-mile days. The latter take a toll on my lower back and feet. Looking down, I see the need for a major retread.

This summer's 49th day passes through exhausting, nearly impregnable acreage, but when the views do emerge, they're winners. Devil's Peak, Crater Lake, Diamond Peak, Mt. McLoughlin, and needle-spired Thielsen — the lightning rod of the Cascades — blossom out.

The closer I climb toward the open sky, the bigger it seems to swell. Crystal clear streams bisect the verdant tarns and are flanked by rocks that resemble fractured molars. Vantage points for the backcountry explorer, from which multitudes of mule deer and whistling, fat marmots can be seen, abound. Hovering hawks take periodic breathers from survival modes to stare you down from close range.

One thicket abounds with pale-green lichen, the internal fiber as coarse as a scouring pad. Many original, rusted-metal emblems remain deeply embedded in tree bark, pinpointing the old Oregon Skyline Trail. Two big bucks now break through the tunneled foliage.

Despite the beauty, sometimes the isolation and raw distances gnaw at me — the emptiness and uncompromising wildness is palpable and chills me at the hollow of my spine.

Since Donner Pass, there have been only three-and-a-half days with accompanying cohorts, so I am ready for a few friendly faces at the upper end of this splendid state. I pay a special meditative eulogy to my dad at Oldenberg Trailhead namesake of his Indiana birthplace. It occurs to me that my ability to orchestrate this run's minute details is an inherited discipline — gleaned from my father whose capacity for organization was boundless.

He was the head accountant for the entire Los Angeles City School System. His compulsive-obsessive German stock planted a stubborn persistence within my spirit. In hundreds of lifetime running events I have dropped out only twice; once with a broken ankle, the other with severe heat stroke that placed me close to death. Such determination I got from him.

I descend gradually onto desert-like terrain, then cross a seasonal creek. The luxuriant green vegetation contrasts with sparsely-needled lodgepole pines covered with their lizard-like bark. How strange it is that nature can allow such discrete landscapes to coexist so peaceably. It must be the effect of the water.

Suddenly it seems the whole earth is quiet. The brushing of my unshaven face against my windbreaker, in the absence of even a breeze rustling the trees, sounds like sandpaper rubbing on rough wood.

After a therapeutic dip in tiny Pinewan Lake, I stumble and fall heavily on a rugged downhill segment just after Crescent Lake. It is only the second tumble since I left the Mexican border. The culprit is a well-camouflaged, debris-covered stump. I gather my pride, grimace at an aching rib cage and kneecap, then shift my weight to the side least traumatized.

The trail passes by some stagnant ponds, then skirts large but shallow Diamond View Lake. Several campsites and swampy flatlands later, I arrive at the headwaters of Trapper Creek, hidden by heavy foliage until now. I meander alongside a host of tempting camps in this shady hemlock haven, but my schedule dictates that I move on.

I round a sharp bend and run smack into three nude trail hikers sporting only their backpacks and boots. The two men look about fortyish with graying sideburns. The woman has chestnut brown hair, braided into a two-foot-long pigtail. She appears to be in her mid-thirties. It is such a shock that I ogle, do a few doubletakes, then muster a polite but feeble greeting. I can't resist discreetly glancing back from a hidden vantage point. Waning sunlight splashes its hues in pastel tones of peach and butterscotch, enhancing those total tans.

Sparkling Heartfelt Camaraderie

Days 108-109 - August 23-24.   While sipping a large Coke and opening a pre-mailed care package at the Odell Lake resort, a stranger places a small bag of food bars, crackers, and wine next to my hip pack. He or she hustles off without waiting to be thanked. Did this person feel sorry for me or just derive great satisfaction from a good samaritan act?

Twilight finds me, because of a chance meeting on a moonlight walk, sharing a campfire sing-along and cinnamon-scented hot apple tarts.

While winding through some of the best backcountry in the world, the trail makes a lasting indentation on my soul. Each day is so different from the next. My developing durability is a precious gift.

Streaking the Pacific Crest Trail   by Mike Dirham

Clearly, no one expects you to run by. I watch their eyes light up and their own personal energy surge as if infected by my enthusiasm. Often they wind up being more excited than I am. Sometimes they take photos or wish autographs. Mostly they seek inspiration.

Former Olympic 10,000-meter runner and 1973 Boston Marathon Champion Jon Anderson arrives at midmorning and drives me down to nearby Eugene. It will be an honor to visit this mystique-filled Oregon town, long a hotbed of distance-running tradition.

Some of the local runners, who've clearly plotted to soothe the effects of my arduous solo jaunt since Crater Lake, are alumni of a seldom held event called the Great Hawaiian Foot Race. This classic covers a half-million meters around Oahu and Maui over a two-week period. Past participants Kip and Jody Leonard open their home for a dramatic reunion. Longtime friends seem to emerge from the woodwork including renowned *Sports Illustrated* writer Kenny Moore.

I feel especially privileged to be recognized with praise and exuberance by so many who have accomplished so much. Personal pride can lead to self-puffery, but I feel embraced by a cadre of beautiful, fit people who exude soothing humility and warmth. I wasn't sure I had earned anything yet, but they, lifting their glasses, respectfully disagreed. It was mighty tough to leave.

Day 110- August 25.   Today Kenny escorts me by car through some of his favorite running turf along the Willamette River. On one cherished 35-mile loop he would consistently grind out a sub-six-minute pace. He was ultimately rewarded with a fourth overall in the marathon at the 1972 Munich Olympics.

At midmorning Kenny points his Volkswagen bug eastward to a trailhead where I will connect with Rob Volkenand, one of Oregon's top ultrarunners, who holds several age-class trail race records.

Bubbling with enthusiasm, Rob shuttles my excess gear to Irish Lake, then darts back toward me on the Pacific Crest Trail. His magnetism draws me toward our meeting at the halfway point.

I chuckle when I find rustic markers placed near tree bottoms, barely one inch above the ground. Clearly this is designed to compensate for downward focus on unpredictable turf as late afternoon fatigue sets in.

A good day's run on great trail is fittingly rewarded by one of Rob's fabulous pasta dishes. It provides a much needed quick-fix of my psychic plumbing. Following a blissful night's rest, my gracious host bids me adieu and drives home to eastern Oregon.

Day 111 - August 26.   Rosary and Waldo lakes are flawlessly handsome on my solo amble through misty rain. I recall thoughts of last night when a star-studded galaxy elicited emotions the angels might share. Today I run through forest gates — wild-eyed and mud-flecked — beside companionable, frosty beargrass. I feel an ongoing interaction with nature's bosom.

Critter chatter is rampant. I no longer feel alone or unacknowledged. Every moment instructs. I revel in my respite from the tight corners of a spaceless society. Right now it is unthinkable that I will return eventually to the land of mechanical toys.

After running for all these hours with two-pound water weights in each hand, I hardly notice their presence during movement. A well-manicured trail encourages me and tailwinds push me to Elk Lake Store, a short distance east of the Pacific Crest Trail. I am at the approximate geographical center of this great state. I celebrate with some involuntary flatulence, the result of an abundance of dried fruit. The store clerk scrutinizes my farting dexterity as if I were a walk-on extra in the movie "Blazing Saddles."

An anti-inflammatory pill, along with twenty minutes of icing, helps soothe my stinging feet in the waning light as waffle layers of clouds scud overhead.

Day 112 - August 27.   Kate and Gary Belanger, fifty percent of my 1985 Sonora Pass support crew, drive in from California to bring me this summer's third pair of shoes. They arrive during a crackling thunderstorm.

Kate prepares a canopy-protected, gourmet extravaganza at a nearby campground while the ear-splitting symphony delivers its ominous message. She will also shuttle around to greet us at the end of our run the next two nights.

Day 113 - August 28.   During some golden morning moments, gritty Gary cajoles me along Sisters Mirror Lake. We dodge a divebombing black crow as we scoot through the lush Three Sisters Wilderness. Upon approaching a hemlock-lined cinder cone named Le Conte Crater, I consider the sequence of events that created this landscape. During research before the run I learned that the original eruption occurred over 5,000 years ago. Later outpourings of hot, basaltic lava ruptured part of the cone's southernmost rim and flowed down a gently undulating, alluvial valley called Wickiup Plain.

A large number of Pacific Crest Trail marker-posts line a lengthy route through stubby knotweed and browning grasses, and leads us just west of a jumbled lava field to the overgrown meadow at Mesa Creek.

South Sister, youngest of the Three Sisters at 10,358 feet, looms imposingly to the northeast. It has erupted three times that we know of and its flanks display over 20 different kinds of volcanic rock.

We pass through shale-like flows and craggy pumice until we are within eyeshot of boulder-lined, 10,047-foot Middle Sister. North Sister, the oldest of the peaks, is still a half an hour ahead of us. North Sister is covered with a series of large scars resulting from glacial activity. The

Backpacking barefoot   by Mike Dirham

Three Sisters area is truly loved as evidenced by the number of campers at this special place. This also means its fragile ecology is increasingly jeopardized. As a result, efforts are under way to restore the land to a near-natural condition.

Smooth, black obsidian rocks and more of the tiny frogs of weeks past line the stark, circuitous tread. It is as if we are trail-skating on thousands of skittish ball bearings. These brittle, glinting shards of volcanic glass clink and crunch in nightmarish harmony.

This afternoon as we romp around a U-shaped contour, we almost run up the heels of a backpacking barefoot woman on a week-long trek in the verdant Sisters environs. She found her boots so ill-fitting and klutzy that she had someone carry them out of the wilderness. A 55-pound pack and thick, leathery calluses had clearly toughened both her feet and mind.

I understand what she did in leaving her boots behind. Embarked on a personal journey, she has altered her physical entrapments for the far greater glory of nature.

A freezing headwind buffets Gary and me in the waning daylight during a laborious crawl over rock-strewn Obbie Dildock Pass. After passing a young group from Colorado, we struggle over a pain-inflicting

Mt. Washington Wilderness   by Kate Belanger

lava field to McKenzie Pass. Just northeast of the pass lies Dee Wright
Observatory. Built of lava blocks, it rises above the ink-black background. Once
inside, each of nearly a dozen windows frames a separate mountain profile.

Tonight's restoration takes place at nearby Lava Lake under a large,
slanted tarp. Fluorescent trails of silver-tinted light sprinkle across an
imposing canopy of lunar dust. I take a gulp of liquid to lubricate a dry
throat. The precious ingredients in my hand-carried bottles serve as my
daily measuring stick of time and life.

I position my spindly frame like a human pretzel as utter fatigue seizes
the backs of my eyelids. I feel a sense of psychological vulnerability to
the elements before I finally drift off.

Day 114 - August 29.   Zero visibility envelopes us at dawn. Miles of
unsteady footing, commencing on the sharp pumice at Belnap Crater's
glaciated basalt flows, make for six bleak hours. When the clouds lift, the
cold and forbidding landscape is a denuded, rutted badland.

Massive sharp rocks stun our toes. We are still being pelted with
precipitation, but a spiritual space suit makes me impervious to the bom-
bardment. Personal effort in the face of these horrendous conditions helps
put a smile on my face and a song in my heart. Whether I feel like smiling
or not, my positive attitude is essential. I am aware that optimism brings
more of the same, and I'm going to need all I can get.

Almost anyone can be a hero for a day; it's hanging in there that
counts. I believe God rewards faithfulness. The long haul is what costs
and counts. We're all in for a long haul in one way or another. For my part,
I'd like to have an interesting one.

God gave a flower perfect discipline. I battle in the rain to attain a
similar quality. This day nature has overpowered me and I feel humbled.

As Gary and I run by glacier-chiseled, 7,794-foot Mt. Washington in
the late afternoon, we have traversed a 65-square-mile lava field that began
at North Sister. We hustle downhill in brown mud to Old Santiam Highway,
then surge across a burn area to Santiam Pass. Finely grained volcanic sand
is strewn with tiny pinecone seeds in this land of charred snags and singed
needles. I find myself beginning to dream of coconut palms and a heat wave.

In embracing this adventure I say "Take me, Earth, and make of me
what you will. My physical discomforts will surely disappear as I become
enveloped in your beauty."

How odd and good it is that negative thoughts that troubled me so
acutely in years past are now trivial.

In recent days I have tried to imagine what I could ever do to match
this experience. I suppose because it is still a story unfolding I won't
envision a greater journey until I have the time and distance to look back
on this one.

So far gone am I now that mere conversation is a chore. When I meet
up with someone, new friend or old, I feel as if I am learning to speak all

over again. The questions I'm expected to respond to, such as "How's it going? What ever made you decide to do this? How do you manage to sleep and eat under such conditions?" often find me producing some canned response because the truth is beyond verbalization. A part of me wants to shout back "Can't you see why I am doing this? Sleeping, eating, and ordinary thought have little to do with all of this." Another part of me says don't answer; if they could understand, they would not ask.

Nonetheless, I force myself to look forward to the next footstrike, the next human encounter. I realize such thoughts and events are critical to my survival at this point. If I cannot share the wisdom I have gained, perhaps I can at least live it.

9 Character Building In Oregon ___

We also come out here to learn about ourselves. The biggest prize in long-distance hiking is the gift of time. Time to look. Time to think. Time to feel. All those hours you spend with your thoughts. You don't solve all of your problems, but you come to understand and accept your-self.

— Cindy Ross
Journey On The Crest

Being a runner by nature, not a hiker, I amend Cindy's words to include long-distance running.

Mother Nature's Frowning Face

Days 115-116 - August 30-31. The brain finally registers that we're smack in the middle of a busy Labor Day weekend. Yesterday, my 114th day, I encountered more hikers than on this summer's previous seven weeks combined.

Labor Day, like Christmas, has clearly lost its original meaning. Holy days and holidays alike have degenerated into just another reason to shop or party. I feel so distant from all of this. I imagine the coolers of Coke and beer in the trunks of cars and in camper kitchens, and wonder what is my place on this earth? I feel marginal apprehension justifying a premature, not yet earned celebration.

I am progressing steadily north since July 5th, yet an elusive Washington border is still ten days away. I feel like a person stuck on the side of a cliff frantically grasping a rope that is their only link to life, unable to visualize anything but the necessary act of holding on. I know that I cannot afford to let go now, figuratively or otherwise. I have even dreamed of waking to find my body muscles, nerves, and brain so out of sync that I cannot rise from the ground. I lie in fear, waiting for a return of known sensation, a lifeline to pull me out.

As the Belangers' depart after three days with me, Pacific Crest Trail hiker and nearby resident Jim Girod steps in as host. He has just taken a five-day breather to recoup from his own ultramarathon walk.

My respite at Jim and Cherie Girod's ranch for two days is incomparable. I truly wonder what I've done to deserve such royal treatment. Their dynamic approach to people is a precious rarity. My ongoing strength of human spirit is a testament to their selfless lifestyle.

Oregon's Three Fingered Jack   by Jim Girod

Day 117 - September 1. At dawn's arrival Jim power walks and I run on a 23-miler to Shale Lake. We are treated on an impeccable day to delightful vistas of Mt. Washington and The Sisters to the south, Broken Top to the north, and Oregon's desert to the east. Electrifying overlooks of emerald basins with their radiant hues punctuate my daydreams.

A southbound hiker warns us of three roaring glacial streams that mercilessly challenged his balance two weeks earlier and also describes a treacherous icy section in his native Washington. But his greatest test came two days out from the Canadian border when he survived a severe nine-hour storm. He attempted to sit it out in a make-shift kitchen-cupboard-sized shelter. His attempts to keep from dozing off in a half-frozen fetal posture nearly proved futile. The raw fear of succumbing to hypothermia affected his ability to move.

I cannot think about sudden squalls or blizzards in unprotected areas ahead for I must give my full effort to today. I have to be mentally "up" each waking hour as it will take thousands of footprints to battle through long hours on my journey north.

Following our lunch stop, Jim hikes while I run on ahead. While alone on several occasions this afternoon, my sense of equilibrium is frozen with anxiety as I cross tricky moderate intensity streams. I clutch at overhead tree limbs with one hand, manipulate a long stick (simulating a third foot) with the other, then inch forward through eddies over moss covered, polished rock.

It is the run's coldest Oregon night. Jim and I arrive separately at Shale Lake and camp well away from water to protect the lakeshore's fragile ecosystem. Before I stop moving around, I put on every layer I've got — both on my torso and extremities — to silence my chattering teeth. We concentrate on replenishing today's heavy fluid loss, caused by perspiration, exhaling moist air, and the chill's diuretic effect. Jim's culinary creation satisfies a pair of massive appetites as we blissfully overcome today's calorie expenditure.

Our bivouac headquarters is situated on high, flat ground, well above gully wind tunnels. A dense forest roof filters the frigid air currents. I place my water bottles inside my bivy sack so they won't freeze. A recent ban on backcountry fires due to drought conditions doesn't help matters as the temperature will drop well below 30 degrees before dawn.

Distant from crowds, I find I am able to grow closer to each individual I encounter. It is as if the intensity of the journey and the constant challenge of mere survival enable me to cut through the usual buffer zone — for trivial chatter has no useful place here.

A solitary beast can be the most sociable of all — I surely am that beast, especially when I see a friendly face on the trail. Without the context of a formal gathering, I am forced to create the setting, whether it be the stump of a log or a country store porch that approximates a homey hearth. Home is wherever I run in these mountains. I no longer feel like an intruder, but a functional part of these environs. Life goes on around me, offering a full spectrum, from the cacophonous glacial stream alongside me approximating the decibel level of a small locomotive to the quiet, curious stares of critters.

Sometimes I just see floppy ears and hear the thump of foot pads, then a blurred exit. A wandering coyote might play at the edge of a low-lying cloud, one step from invisibility. Elk would run into the mist and disappear with the ground continuing to tremble after they have moved out of sight. A bear sow might stand on rear legs to get a better look at me before smashing off into the forest. I am mesmerized by the glimpses of cuddly wild things like the treebound cubs further south.

Forested corridors bisect the barely disturbed contour of the land. I learn to discern the shape of the slope, rocks, and trees while enshrouded in mountain fog.

The depth of the run itself blends with the integrity of a natural world and my place in it. A life needs direction and this ribbon I follow is precisely where I might choose to spend the rest of it. Rather than enshroud myself in a fog of personal concerns, I focus on the experience, not just prearranged mileage goals.

Life is a struggle with limits and occasionally we need to test them to find out who we are. Running in the wild provides a simple source of happiness, but doesn't always dole out pleasure. You have to believe you can do it. Your priorities have got to be in order. Some days are far tougher than others. The discipline of mastering a worthwhile challenge shapes and strengthens with a spiritual bonding.

More Gardens of Eden

Day 118 - September 2.   It takes a full 30 minutes at dawn for Jim and I to defrost our bodies and warm our clothes on flat sunbathed rocks. I fold my clothes and fastidiously tighten them with thick rubber bands. This enables a snug fit of my pack.

Today Jim officiates as my wilderness steward as we thread our way into his favorite backyard, Jefferson Park. Explorers Lewis and Clark named the park after our third president around 1800.

A dangerous crossing of milky, raging Russell Creek gets our undivided attention. The picturesque setting at blue-green Scout Lake, shadowed by the changing moods of 10,495-foot Mt. Jefferson, offers lasting impressions. All of us need beauty as well as bread, and we are treated to unlimited visual packages here. Jim points out a spectacular lookout point as we indulge ourselves with nearby huckleberries.

Today's grinding 24-miler gravitates us down through a mile-long forest to an aquamarine gem called Olallie Lake where we homestead until dawn.

Day 119 - September 3.   Jim and I part for we have separate destination goals and time schedules, but we will connect one more time just south of Mt. Hood, Oregon's highest peak.

On I go. Sounds of water and wind, smells of damp earth, solitude, scenery, and swim stops enhance this solo 30-miler. I drink in luxuriant waterfalls and lucent pools. Sheer canyon walls stand guard over a breathtaking trail blasted through solid rock. I run over a perfectly engineered wooden bridge that spans Warm Springs Creek. I scratch out a note of appreciation for Jim which I leave under a large prominent rock.

At twilight I pull into Clackamas Guard Station to munch a light bite and bed down.

If I do not pay close attention to my nutritional needs I know I will never reach Canada. Several tasty, high carbo-laden PowerBars during the running hours effectively uplift my morale. The fructose and maltodextrin ingredients sustain my energy, are easily digestible, and satisfy my hunger for long periods of time. I find these bars provide the greatest endurance results of any food product I have ever used.

I also mix Bodyfuel, a powdered carbo-loading pick-up, with fluids daily. It increases my overall performance level, especially on long, steep grades at altitude. Each ration is separately packaged in a small plastic envelope.

Although this is decidedly a no-frills trail jaunt, I eliminate any masochistic tendencies by interjecting hot meals, a shower, and a few beers on rest days. My ever-present bottomless pit could be counted on to help me regain lost weight.

Twice I have served as a running postman, delivering mail between backcountry ranger stations and picking up trash along the way. I welcome these opportunities because they put me back in touch with the world at large without infringing on my private journey.

Day 120 - September 4. I begin a crushing marathon push over Wapinita and Barlow passes. A brief but stiffening submergence in 42-degree Little Crater Lake refreshes me at midday.

Today's mileage overdose has me running below the southern perimeter of multi-glaciered, 11,245-foot Mt. Hood which erupted about 1,500 years ago. I am flabbergasted as two elderly female hikers present me with a picture-perfect red apple and individual kisses on the cheek. The juicy piece of fruit falls just slightly short of matching the color in my blushing cheeks.

Later in the day I maneuver soberly across two churning stream chasms. The roily torrent comes right off a massive glacier and hurdles over rock at colossal speed. Both crossings nearly deafen me as the facing canyons vibrate and roar. Just above the second span, a pounding waterfall penetrates this jumbled land of broken stone like a cylindrical torpedo. Laden with silt and powdery clay, the water appears polluted. But this far from the sins of the masses, I don't believe that's really the case.

Ideally, these pulsating fords should be traversed early in the day when the water is usually at its lowest point and calmest. By early afternoon the sun has melted large slabs of thick ice, and a low key flow can become a tumultuous wild river.

During the next two miles I struggle through a section of wearisome sand.

As I close the distance on majestic Mt. Hood, I contemplate upon the mighty forces that nature places upon the land and all that pass through it. Winter whiteout conditions that have led to numerous fatalities here. Avalanches are also a hazard. Climbers often attempt to reach Mt. Hood's alluring but treacherous summit by sunrise, to combat the avalanche dangers created by rapidly melting snow. And the powerful glaciers chew up vast chunks of the mountain while leaving permanent scars.

I finally arrive at Timberline Lodge, a sturdily built stone and wood fortress dating back to the depression era. It takes me a full 20 minutes to scrape the caked dirt and crud off my body. I rejoice with some sandwiches and a large pitcher of frosty brew. To my mind, the ice-cold ingredients are a stalwart member of America's fifth food group.

Days 121-122 - September 5-6.   On the first of two rest days, I run back out and pace Jim in. I revel at being caught up in the lovely Oregonian philosophy where caring people look out for each other on well-manicured trails.

In the morning Jim walks north toward Washington. Court and Janis Mumford, longtime friends, drive in from their home in Portland, several hours away. An accomplished ultra-endurance athlete, Court will join me on the trail for what will turn out to be a harrowing two-day experience.

Hood Is Good, But Not At Night

> *The difficult we do immediately. The impossible takes a little longer.*
>
> — Slogan for U.S. Army Service Forces

Days 123-124 - September 7-8.   This summer's final spree is about to be numbed by deteriorating weather.

The combination of a poorly signed trail and a hasty choice will heave us well into darkness. Court tells the story best in his recap of the traumatic episode:

> "The night we met Bob at Timberline Lodge was his 122nd in the wilderness. My wife Janis and I drove to Mt. Hood from Portland that afternoon, arriving to a gorgeous and inspiring sunset.
>
> The three of us, four if you count our wolfdog Esther, paused to enjoy this spectacular setting from the stone terrace of the lodge. We were leaving to find more financially hospitable accommodations.

Mazama Lodge was difficult to find, but the trouble was well worth it. Somewhat spartan by comparison to the Timberline, it was rustic and warm with a large crackling fire under the huge stone hearth. Our greeting was very friendly and the price was a marked improvement. As a bonus there was even a warm buffet waiting.

Up early the next morning, we were ready for the trail. After a large breakfast of fresh huckleberry hotcakes we drove back up to the Timberline Lodge where the Pacific Crest Trail and the Mt. Hood Paradise Trail are one and the same.

In the early morning sun, under an unblemished blue sky, Janis took a bon voyage photo on the trail. Water bottles full and secure, iodine tablets and fanny pack supplies in place, we set off to Esther's howl. Thus commenced one of the most memorable days of running I've experienced. The scenery was ever changing, from lush green forest vistas to an enshrouded wooded wonderland, from an immense flowing meadow of colorful wild flowers to an intimate waterfall; all the while a continually changing perspective of magnificently awesome Mt. Hood and its mighty glaciers flooded in brilliant sunshine. Our running pace, though not fast, was consistent.

You must cross the creeks that accommodate glacial run-off before midday when they become rivers. This was important. Not so important, however, that one doesn't take time to greet hikers on the trail. Bob Holtel is used to that. And used to the inquisitive response he receives when it is divulged that he is running the entire Pacific Crest Trail. I accompany him on the last two days of his second summer on the trail.

Another diversion worthy of time were the notes written and deposited in various places by hikers and their comrades. A few fun notes were for Bob, left earlier by Pacific Crest Trail hiker Jim Girod.

Once Sandy Creek was successfully forded, a slightly harrowing experience, we were at ease to let the miles come at whatever pace. We exchanged the lead many times. Although conversation was plentiful, much of the time we ran in silence, individually with the trail. Press-

This is what wilderness running is all about   by Janis Mumford

ing further north around Mt. Hood, after the Pacific Crest Trail leaves the circular Paradise Trail, we saw few hikers.

I was impressed by Bob's knowledge of what we were seeing as well as what was coming up. I began to appreciate the kind of planning required of this venture. Bob paraphrased Jay Birmingham's motivational words, 'dream, plan, endure, achieve.'

I learned of the excellent reference book he used, *The Pacific Crest Trail* by Jeff Schaffer and others. Its information proved very useful.

After some 25 miles of running we came to the junction for the Huckleberry Trail to Lost Lake. Being a bit ahead I decided to sit on a log and wait. When Bob arrived he hollered, 'What's this?' upon spotting an arrow and writing in the dirt. 'It says: Lost Lake, Court and Bob. Ah, Janis and Esther have already been here.' They had driven around the mountain, set up camp, and hiked in to leave us an inspirational sign. I leaped up and we bounded down the trail toward Lost Lake.

Lost Lake is a beautiful spot, with excellent facilities, adjacent to the north slope of Mt. Hood. Arriving at the campsite, post haste, Bob and I downed a brew or two and

built a fire. We then enjoyed one of Janis' terrific —
gourmet — Pritikin dinners by candlelight. A terrific way
to end a wonderful day.

I awoke in the night to the howl of the wind. The temperature had dropped appreciably and I heard thunder in the
distance. Weather changes quickly in the mountains. At
dawn my fears were realized. There was cold rain and the
wind was blowing hard. Hot coffee and some fantastic
mountain mush, along with plenty of layers of clothing,
took the chill off.

After this breakfast feast we were ready to set out. Bob
started with long pants, but I figured I'd be okay in shorts
once we got moving. I also had on four layers of cotton,
including a hooded sweatshirt, and a nylon windshell. Not
ideal, but I suspected adequate. The first couple of miles
back up to the Pacific Crest Trail were just that — up.
How better to get the body fuel and heater working. I knew
that going up also meant going into the moist clouds.

The rush of the wind became louder as we climbed from
the lake valley. No matter, the trail was wooded, hence
protected. If we kept running, the cold would not be a
problem. Wet shoes gave way to soaked feet. We traversed
several ridges, never leaving the elevation of the clouds.
It wasn't getting any warmer or drier.

Occasionally the ridge would become exposed to the south,
the direction of the weather. That made it very cold. Some
of the trail was across lava flows. That made it very slow.
Some of the trail was both. I kept hoping to descend or at
least have back our lovely soft trail. Instead it was this
loose lava trail and blasting, bitter-cold wind and rain.
Uck! As the degree of difficulty peaked, the trail became
so exposed to the howling weather and the footing so
rocky that it seemed it couldn't have worsened.

We finally arrived at a junction. A note left on the trail
sign greeted us: 'The last few miles of trail are shit!' It
was signed by Jim Girod.

But we could now get off this ridge. The next bit of track,
very lush, beautiful, and protected, was pure ecstasy. It
took us to the Eagle Creek Trail, and after four-plus

hours on the ridge it was wonderful to go down, out of the clouds.

Eagle Creek empties into the Columbia near Cascade Locks. This section has a splendor usually seen in *National Geographic*. After some 20 miles of wet and cold running, to come upon this sight completely erased any fragments of negative thinking from the earlier experience. No matter that it was raining, we were in a very special place. Our pace slowed, indeed often stopped, to enjoy this treasure of magnificent waterfalls, clear and deep pools, fern-covered cliffs, spectacular gorges, tranquil ponds, and beautiful woods. It was all here; bombarding every sense of the imagination. The trail was once again soft and welcoming.

It was late in the afternoon when we could first see the mighty Columbia River. At that time the rain became torrential. If we were to take the direct route, the Old Columbia Gorge Highway, we were fairly close to our destination. On the trail, the purest route, it would be just over twice as far and infinitely more scenic. We were anxious to get back into the woods anyway. So obviously it was press on.

We felt we had 4-1/2 miles on Ruckle Creek Trail to the Bridge of the Gods, our terminus and the conclusion of Bob's 66th day this summer.

The trail went directly UP. And up and Up and UP. As the rain abated we stopped once for me to let my heart sink back into my chest, to eat what was left of the energy bars, drink some water, and enjoy the vista from high above the river. Then it was back to steeper uphill running than I've ever experienced, but we knew we had just a few miles to go.

Finally we reached a plateau where we were sure the trail would then cut back north. But trails do what they do, and we kept going east and up. How can this be, we wondered? Surely we've gone four or five miles. I hated to mention it to Bob, but we had perhaps just one more hour of daylight. Though it had already been a long day, our pace quickened. It was hardly raining now but we were still soaked. Wouldn't this trail please turn north?

A rule of trail running, indeed of survival, is never leave the trail. As dusk settled in, it was becoming increasingly difficult just to see it. Right after dark, we finally came to a junction with the sign: Pacific Crest Trail to Cascade Locks: 9 miles! Our worst fears were realized. We had doubled back on Ruckle Creek Trail. So there we were, at dark, with nine miles still to run.

Poor Janis, I thought, she'll be worried sick.

Although we had expected to be finished long before dark, Bob, being ever prepared, produced the smallest of flashlights. As long as we kept moving we could stay warm. As long as the critical beam kept working, we could make our way.

At first it seemed awkward, as it was pitch black in the forest on this overcast night. It took some experimenting to determine the best way to shine the light for both of us to see. What seemed to work best was for me to run in the front, carry the light, and shine it down at my feet. Bob, one step behind, could then see his footing. Of course, our progress was dependent on the flashlight working.

We were doing just fine. The trail was leading us on a most circuitous route in and out of the deep forest, but we knew

Happy Author (rt) and Court Mumford prior to late night vigil   by Janis Mumford

we were on the right path, headed north and west. And Bob would say, 'Just keep moving, endure, be patient, and pray for the flashlight.'

At once it happened, the unthinkable. The son-of-a-gun blinked. What was that? Bob reported that he had just replaced the batteries and bulb, but again it blinked. Then it was black. Everywhere. Pitch black.

Threatening it with expletives didn't help, nor did banging it on the palm of my hand. Bob was verbally angered at all mechanical and electrical things in the world — 'they always let you down.' Old engineer Court was taking the damn thing apart by braille, rearranging the batteries, wiggling the spring, anything. All the while we were trying to press on.

For some unexplained reason the light did come back on briefly, at which time we tripled our pace. Not a major feat, considering how slow we were moving. But then it would go out again, so it became place-and-test-each-step-one-foot-at-a-time. This was going to be a very, very long night. Poor Janis.

Once removed from the setting, it could have appeared comical. Our most efficient method was for Bob to literally hang onto my butt pack while I groped for the trail. The groping was at a snail's pace and somewhat danger-ous, but we found it possible to keep moving. For one thing, the trail had a distinguishable pitch. Also, wearing shorts, it was immediately obvious when we got off the trail and into the bushes or rock. To my surprise the trail appeared as the darkest part of the all-black surroundings, unless that bleakest part just happened to be a tree. In that case, we would walk directly into the tree.

I discovered that by unscrewing the flashlight, when I'd screw it together again, we got a couple of seconds of light. It was definitely worth the effort. So this is the way we traveled over the next few miles. We'd step and test to see if it felt like the trail. Twist for a glimmer of light and watch out for roots, rocks, and bushes. 'You okay?' 'Okay!'

Bob lamented somewhere along the way that in his expe-rience on the Pacific Crest Trail he'd learned how appropriate was the 'Crest' part of its name, which it continually stays on. Below we could see the lights of Cascade Locks, but we weren't going down. Instead, we were weaving around the convolutions of the gorge, in and out, round about, but not down. It was frustrating, but we were inching along slowly. Movement was important as the night was still wet and cold. We were making progress, but it was quite late. Poor Janis.

Occasionally our spirits would wane, like the time we thought we'd traveled a spur to a dead-end overlook. Thank Bob for feeling out the trail which had taken a characteristic switchback.

Finally starting down, the trail goes into the deepest of black forest. After a couple of flirtations with the ledge, one direct hit by a tree, and my head-first fall over some rocks, we came upon a footbridge. Our sense antenna fully extended, we stopped to discuss this apparition in the darkened wilderness. What was it, we pondered, though not for long. Very cautiously we chanced this bridge and to our amazement a road lay just across. A one-lane dirt road to us resembled a major freeway. But here it was and going in the right direction.

It wasn't long, maybe two miles down this wonderful road, when we emerged on a back street in sleepy Cascade Locks. It was something like 1:30 a.m. and not a creature was stirring, save two, and no telling what we looked like. We walked toward the center of town until the sole moving vehicle came into sight. Running and waving to intercept it we realized it was the local police who had spotted us. On approaching, the policeman rolled down his window, smiled, and said: 'I was wondering if we were going to find you two tonight. I'll call Janis!'

I turned to Bob, smiling, 'Tell me again what comes after endure?'"

My only major wrong turn since Mexico was to somehow misinterpret the ambiguous Ruckle Creek Junction. I am not proud of that error. It vented forth when I neglected to double check the topo in harsh rain. The ensuing ordeal created a low point in the run and inconvenienced my compatriots. It put a damper on any subsequent revelry. Nonetheless, I utter a prayer of appreciation that a greater mishap did not occur.

A Cascades panorama   by Lee Freeman

I squirm inwardly as I vow diligence in preventing a similar episode in Washington's boggy, even more remote Cascades.

In nearby Portland, Court and Janis offer a hot meal and a soft bed. Their hospitality eases the disheartening culture shock of my return to urban environs. In some ways it seems a fitting end to this segment. I feel like this summer's adventure terminated like a severely blown flat tire. My human fallibility embarrassed me to friends and acquaintances. However, I feel a whole lot better when I consider the successes gleaned over the other 65 days. If I were a perfectionist, I might have abandoned ship right there. I would have ample time to think things out and rise above this deep pool of damaged pride.

I cannot help but anticipate my callousness toward hometown congested roads. I will once again see those harried, sedentary drivers stuffed into high-tech vehicles and honking their horns at the slightest provocation. I will inevitably hear their piercing car alarms when they park. I am not too anxious to re-enter the real world as a participating entity. I already know what is there.

Summer of '87
Columbia River Gorge
to Canada

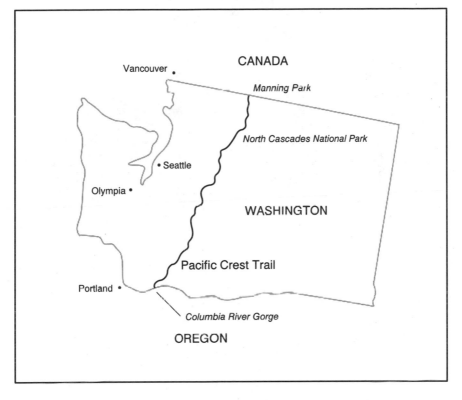

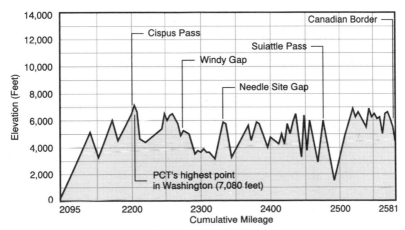

Bridge of the Gods across the Columbia River   by Janis Mumford

10 In God's Hands _____

*Simplicity in all things is the secret of the wilderness and
one of its most valuable lessons. It is what we leave
behind that is important. I think the matter of simplicity
goes further than just food, equipment, and unnecessary
gadgets; it goes into the matter of thoughts and objectives
as well. When in the wilds, we must not carry our problems with us or the joy is lost.*

— Sigurd Olson
Reflections From The North Country

The 66-day run through Northern California and Oregon the previous
summer was, in fact, tainted with uneasiness. When I got back to Manhattan Beach I went over my notes and reviewed with some of my running
friends what happened. From reading the last few chapters, you probably
would conclude that it was a masterpiece of planning and execution —
an adventure of which my German forebears would be proud. Well, it
wasn't.

I knew things were not going well last summer, but I did not allow
myself to even think about stopping. I had exposed myself and some of
my friends to dangerous situations. I knew what was wrong. I hadn't
prepared diligently enough. I had not contacted enough people along my
route. I had not realized that the farther I got from home base the greater
the overall risk. So I set about correcting things.

Wilderness running naturally entails enough uncontrollable risk. It is
inexcusable not to account for the controllable risk. For example, during
the second summer there were over 50 days of running solo. That is not
good planning. Visions of broken bones, freezing nights, and days without
food flashed through my mind.

Turning It Around

This is July 20, 1987. After ten months in the jungle of hard surfaces,
motorized transit, and early morning coffee (one of the better aspects of
civilization), I am back at the Mumford residence in Portland for pre-trail
carbo-loading.

To prepare for this third summer, I tried to upgrade mental toughness
by intensifying my physical disciplines. I strengthened my legs with hill
running and long stretches of soft sand. I learned if the quads get thrashed,
the knee will inherit most of the torque. Any weakness encourages injury
when you are moving fast, and downhill, out of control.

After a long trail run I would elevate my legs against a tree to drain accumulated natural wastes and alleviate foot swelling.

I'd swim in the ocean and fresh water ponds year round to brace for daily high altitude bathing. I would drive to the mountain ranges near my home, then romp to the top to acclimate. An ample regimen of pushups and situps strengthened my arm and stomach muscles.

I read everything I could get my hands on about hypothermia, stream crossings, and compass techniques when no landmarks are visible. I felt this was necessary because of Washington's perennial wetness, windchill, and limited visibility, are exacerbated by dangerous, quick-hitting Cascade storms. The majority of our country's glaciers (excluding Alaska) are found in this state. As they melt, already hazardous knee-to-waist-deep river crossings become faster and deeper. My plans called for locating the widest spot, which is usually the shallowest and slowest, before attempting to cross.

I had special UVA lenses set into sunglasses to deter glare and possible snow-blindness. Sunburning of the eyeball has forced many ill-prepared hikers out of the mountains.

Lastly, I memorized numerous inspirational readings and motivational tapes to enhance an already strong Christian spirit.

Trail Angels

Day 125 - July 22.   The third-summer finale commences today as the ever-gracious Mumfords warm me with good luck embraces at the Columbia Gorge, lowest point on the Pacific Crest Trail. Court and Janis reluctantly depart with big grins and vigorous arm waving.

Two-time Crater Lake marathon champ Martin Balding, a longtime California friend, steps in to squire me across the Bridge of the Gods from Cascade Locks, Oregon to Stevenson, Washington.

After tightrope walking along the two-foot shoulder of a truck-laden Washington thoroughfare in lieu of a short section of uncompleted trail at this date, we pick up Wayne Harpel, a distance runner who works for the U.S. Forest Service near Mount St. Helens. His expertise on resupply arteries and escape routes proves invaluable. Both their wives would aid us once or twice daily, for five days, at periodic road crossings.

As a running trio, Martin, Wayne, and I master the stoic trudge around Big Huckleberry Mountain in a heavy drizzle while wading through huge outcrops of body-blanching vegetation, too dense for comfortable passage. Northern Cascade squalls have us feeling as if we are imprisoned within a moving, outdoor automatic car wash. Erratic winds whistle up my Gore-Tex jacket.

Succulent thimbleberries, decorating gangly stalks, fuel the system along with PowerBars and trail mix as we thaw out at bone-dry Crest Camp. An abundance of marionberries, salmonberries, raspberries, huckleberries, blackberries, and wild strawberries will bring treasured culinary experiences for several days to come.

We seem to be getting a glimpse of a wetter, and perhaps, wilder land beyond. But Janet Balding and Judi Harpel's congenial guardianship softens our moods, aching muscles, and doctored blisters.

Tonight, I sleep swaddled beneath a supple umbrella of bent pine; three large trees twisted together create a natural, storm-shunting barrier. Slumber is broken only once when the air rings with the distant mating sounds of a bull elk bugling to his harem.

Day 126 - July 23.   A nearly horizontal, gust-driven hailstorm galvanizes us as we stagger through Indian Heaven Wilderness past Blue, Bear, and Deer lakes in strained pursuit of Steamboat Lake. We traverse a ridge plush with ferns, moss, and small roots. Half the time the trail is covered with tall grass, the remainder littered with broken stone. The track now steepens and meanders through an open, silent forest toward fog-shrouded hillsides of switchbacking talus.

A drenched chipmunk, all stripes, fuzz, and muscle, cocks his head, quivers, and sprints for cover. A sporadic ray of light filters through the billowing canopy onto the forest floor as Martin, Wayne, and I squish on. Mist glistens on our trash bag raincoats and shines on the fur of pikas and marmots as they whistle at us.

We learn it is prudent to keep going during periods of freezing rain. Eventually, the storm passes and gorgeous weather makes it all worthwhile. At various high points I even sing to the trees and the birds sing back. Everytime we cross a huge alpine meadow I feel somewhat like I am running through Heaven's gate.

A sedating afternoon pond dip restores our cleanliness while nearby a long line of trees shades our campsite under marching clouds. A skittish wind sends shimmering white sparks streaming over the pond surface like a squadron of small hummingbirds. Tonight the evening light sweeps across the ridges, gleaning silver from the moon, and the day's precipitation is easily forgotten.

The first couple of nights back on the trail I experience some difficulty adjusting to the routine, but it soon becomes second nature. A most critical step is to disguise my fanny pack as a pillow at night. With minimal food smells inside, I don't have to hang its contents in stuff bags from a tree limb. I hope that bears will be attracted to much larger backpacker packs which hold infinitely more promise. I am not harassed once.

I discretely bury all body waste in rock-dug holes well away from streambeds. I leave no identifying toilet paper flags.

Day 127 - July 24.   A bold, frisky jaybird plucks a dried banana slice right out of my granola as I watch dawn unfold from a shoreline tree stump. Squirrels and mice steal us blind. They are brazen, determined, and attack our food with a kamikaze mentality. A whipping, ever-thickening swirl of intermittent fog creates ghostly shadows against the July sky. A one-hour downpour pelts us without pity and flash floods everything as we quickly opt for any available rock overhang or hollowed out tree trunk.

A glorious transfixing sun breaks through to roust the hillsides and bolster our spirits. We find ourselves splashing along a mystical garden on the ten-mile western arm of 12,276-foot Mt. Adams. The trail holds an almost level contour just above timberline. This gigantic sub-alpine paradise headlines endless lupine, Indian paintbrush, monkey flower, columbine, fireweed, marigold, white tiger lily, and tall beargrass, all brilliantly illuminated by the warm-day sun. Nestled amongst this enchanting festoon lie diminutive smaller blooms, some the size of a fingernail. I am awestruck at seeing life so delicate sprouting from terrain so rugged. The brilliant colors make one forget everything that hurts.

I had spent two weeks earlier this month in California's High Sierra at 10,000 feet injecting a random sprinkling of hazardous stream fords into five-hour runs while a guest at John Cosgrove's Mammoth Athletic Camp. That practice pays off with today's trembling, but successful log crossing high above the nasty, roaring Middle Fork of Adams Creek.

We edge around a two-foot-long, brownish-black porcupine that dominates the tread on a sharp turn. Its back and tail are covered with strong, stiff quills. When defending themselves, their barbed tips penetrate flesh like miniature darts. Predators sometimes attempt to flip them over; they are quite vulnerable belly up. Porcupines inadvertently kill young trees by stripping bark indiscriminately. Once around we move on.

Marmots basking on a glacial boulder shelf eye us curiously as the rustling of aspens in the background lull the senses. I am touched by the glistening greens and warm ambers, as gentle breezes drop down to caress us.

We stop in our tracks on spotting a grand lunch spot just below a waterfall on meandering Killen Creek. A gargantuan-tentacled tree provides an ornate rain shelter. I attempt to use a rotting log for a balance beam and it crumbles underfoot. I spot several goats grazing on sparse vegetation on a craggy mesa. This visceral interaction with the land and the animals sharpens my sense of purpose.

After an invigorating rinse at Lava Spring, a brooding stillness is broken by earsplitting yells and motor boats on nearby Horseshoe Lake.

We have completed almost 90 miles in three days. I savor the cradling warmth of each transitory moment. I feel frugal and free. The night stays clear and windless as we rest supine on the soft earth, a peaceful distance from the lakeshore hubbub.

I daydream as I lie in my bivy and watch a massive moon rise. The lake mirrors the mountains as radiantly as a picture calendar. Symphonies of thought drift into the chasms of my soul, warming my restless heart. I take in the pleasant moments of the day, rather than dwell on tomorrow's anxieties.

Porcupine hinders progress   by Mike Dirham

Galloping Through Goat Rocks With Guarded Gusto

Day 128 - July 25.   After eating cold granola we charge north, the
Pacific Crest Trail sweeping us around a symmetrically near-perfect pine
tree bowl. Fingers of sunlight play over tiny moss-rich rivulets like spokes
on a wheel. The basin cradles pristine Walupt Lake with Mt. Adams acting
as an alert, backwoods overseer. We dart among scrub pines, dash over
polished granite, and bark out short bursts of joy that are lost in the wind.
This pastoral blanket has miraculously escaped any clearcut scars.

The skyline at Cispus Pass is electrifying. Here nature proudly dis-
plays Goat Rocks with its medley of pinnacles, accentuated by a heart-
thumping traverse across the glistening flank of white-mantled Old Snowy
Mountain. Near its top we reach the Pacific Crest Trail's highest point in
Washington — 7,080 feet — culminating a 1,400-foot climb.

I sometimes run faster uphill than on the level or downgrade. An early history of ego-bruising, face-planting falls have softened both my thinking and my pace on trail descents.

One achieves a joint-shattering impact ratio of three times your body weight, placed squarely upon the 52 bones of your feet, while plummeting from a summit notch to a distant canyon bottom. Conversely, the shock absorption ratio on lung-searing uphill grinds is far less.

I am in complete harmony with the wild. All I need for survival is stowed on my hips or in my head. I may never again achieve a life of such innocent simplicity.

Today's air is heavy with the scent of pitch as we zigzag over a wonderful carpet strewn with pine cones and polished stone. Each day seems to unfold wilder and more resplendent than the day before. Although I have been blessed over the years with the opportunity to experience firsthand much of the world's natural beauty, I wonder whether there's a place on earth that can match the Cascades for sheer ruggedness and wonderment.

We climax todays 24-miler by dropping to Bypass Camp located within the irresistible drawstring of a minareted colonnade. Each night's respite finds us in a spectacular new spot.

This evening, individually tiered, natural flat shelves, amid enshrouding pines create a blissful bivouac. My quivering, rubbery legs battle to relax from the hours of pure uphill exhaustion and the hours of countless switchbacks.

Safety in Numbers

Day 129 - July 26. Our fifth dawn together commences a comparatively short but fearful 20-miler down to White Pass. We are immediately enveloped by the musky odors of sun-warmed grass and scents of rich pine resin. The air is cold, thin, and sterile in this land of scree slopes, glacial tarns, and pocket-sized ponds.

Once again we are pitted against nature at its most powerful. This day will prove far more trying than initially anticipated.

I know that you can't run well with an ice ax and crampons which can cause you to stumble or trip. As a result, I carry neither.

I make sure I have at least one pacer in reputedly steep, icy areas, where an unarrested fall can have serious consequences. On extremely harrowing slopes, footing can be treacherous due to the snow becoming hard and slick during certain time periods. If necessary we will tie ourselves together with a light rope for safety, then hammer our waffle soles into the encrusted snowbank to create maximum traction. For protection should we fall, we will cover all exposed skin with clothing.

We are now running through some of the most spectacular scenery in the continental United States. High peaks, huge glaciers, and sheer, intimidating walls are everywhere.

Within minutes we are clattering across the tops of crusty suncups. I feel like I am walking over a giant cheese grater. The sound is that of crinkling plastic. We tie ourselves together for 300 yards across steep Packwood Glacier. Not one of us speaks a word. Our white-knuckled fingers shake and throb throughout the crossing. The painstakingly meticulous traverse is successful. Life is unpredictable, but a watchful God is with us!

The Pacific Crest Trail now makes a spinning ramble down a series of precipitous ledges and then along a knife-edged backbone. We thread the crest for two miles in gusting winds. Foreboding drops approach 1,500 feet on either side. I am tightrope walking along an aerial passageway without a hatch door handle to get a grip on. Crumbly, cliffside footing controls any thoughts of recklessness. Courage, I realize, is fear that has said its prayers. One slip and it is a long, treacherous slide to the bottom. I solemnly utter several silent requests today.

We carom like pinballs toward the ski resort at White Pass to thaw out bones and soothe twitching muscles. I fully realize that the unpretentious Balding and Harpel families, who on four consecutive days greeted us with shuttled-in meals, temporary shelter, and comradeship, are the consummate heroes of these 134 miles.

Fun Time

Day 130-131 - July 27-28. We find ourselves flanked by 54 teenage participants of a mountain running camp and their coaches. When I divulge my destination and how I'm getting there, I am asked to give an after-dinner talk to the coed contingent in exchange for a bunk. Unfortunately, their liability conscious director gruffly disallows both. I wondered what possible danger might transpire. Apparently he was focusing on the risk if I fell out of bed or cracked a toe in the dormitory darkness.

We head for the more amiable atmosphere of a small foothill cafe. Invariably these casual eateries combine inexpensive homemade meals with country warmth and contagious smiles. Following four or five consecutive high-mileage days I would excitedly approach a trailhead primed to rub shoulders with this friendliness. Attitude is almost everything.

My care packages that arrive early are held over by congenial rural postmasters even though their storage space is limited. The key phrase "PLEASE HOLD FOR PACIFIC CREST RUNNER," accompanied by my anticipated arrival date, is on each. This proves very effective. I just had to make sure I timed my town visits when the post office was open.

Some lodges and guard stations, acting as temporary post offices, were closed when I ran in. This created the awkward task of finding someone reasonably official to help me retrieve the caches. The dried foods inside, bland though they became, were critical to my survival for the 110 trail days I subsisted on them.

Rest stop between White and Chinook passes   by Kent Holder

After a fantastic family-style pasta dinner I am driven down the west side of White Pass to the wholesome hamlet of Packwood. After the Balding-Harpel entourage bids me adieu, I shower, shave, and prepare to bed down in a ranger station barracks.

Lary Webster, superb Washington ultrarunner, motors in from Seattle to visit and eventually return me to the trailhead.

Huntington Beach Fireman Kent Holder and his wife Ann, longtime friends, have just driven 1,100 miles from Southern California. Kent has paced aforementioned blind athlete Harry Cordellos to many record-breaking performances, and is an outstanding 50 and 100-mile runner himself. Ann was recently selected "Teacher of the Year" in her school district. A Higher Power may have permanently discarded the mold right after creating these two selfless, caring human beings.

Mother Nature Frowns and Other Horrors

Day 132 - July 29. Kent, Lary, and I run alongside Deer and Dumbbell lakes. We pause to munch a PowerBar on the irregular grass at Crag Lake's upper lip.

Mushrooms, slimy banana slugs, animal hair, deer scat, bird feathers, and small bone fragments periodically dot the trail. Several clusters of the latter offer evidence of at least one forest creature's recent meal. I am reminded of how different nature's behavioral codes are from man's. When humans kill one another, it is rarely for survival. How ironic and awful that in war such killing is sanctioned and in (relative) peacetime, forbidden. I wonder who'd be left on earth if nature were to intervene and establish her priorities as our governing guidelines. Hopefully, I would still be around.

Huge stands of pine and fir skirt neatly stacked boulders for as far as the eye can see. This myriad of lushness, so blessedly green that I ache with joy, is suddenly swept clear of clouds by a fresh breeze. The distinctive rugged setting, with its thin air and cold chill, contrasts sharply with the muted foothills and lower elevation valleys. Fallen, first-growth trees abound as the badly eroded trail, no more than a foot wide, leaves much to be desired. I realize this is part of the price for being allowed into such a special secret place. The beauty is a reward in itself, and I suddenly find myself communicating my delight by caressing a geriatric tree.

After taking in Mt. Rainier's dynamic beauty from many viewpoints on this 28-mile day, with upbeat spirits, six sorely pounded lower limbs head down to Chinook Pass. Lary departs, and the Holders and I psyche up for a well earned rest day.

Day 133 - July 30.   Lightning cracks on the distant crags. It rains part of the afternoon, all night, and well into dawn, making it difficult to face the long day ahead.

Day 134   July 31.   Kent and I, two soundly drenched stick figures, span Bear Gap, then skirt two heavily wooded rectangular basins on rugged switchbacks. I jam one toe on a hidden stump that blends in perfectly with the mud-flecked terrain. My frame hurtles out of control into an ungraceful one-point landing on my right rib cage. Nothing is cracked, but the resulting tenderness will cause lingering torment for the next 48 hours — especially when I'm running, bending to tie a shoelace, or changing positions while sleeping.

Meanwhile, Ann has driven the Holders' 4WD camper/pickup truck over a spaghetti network of rock-strewn, Forest Service fire roads. Her incredible backcountry instincts miraculously position her within a half-mile of today's destination, a large, one-room cabin at Camp Urich.

Upon arrival we scrape coyote scat, that contains fur from small rodents, from the cabin entrance. Next to the coyote residue we see a decaying pile of tallow-smeared bones. They show the scoring imprints of a predator's teeth, the results of a violent, one-sided skirmish.

One of Ann's special hot pasta and veggie dishes helps massage our spirits. At an after-dinner campfire I accidentally split off a good chunk of one front tooth during some vigorous toothpick activity. Physical anguish is minimal, but the grotesque, gaping hole peers through a clammy, unshaven backdrop.

One of the better signs on the Pacific Crest Trail   by Kent Holder

Day 135 - August 1. At dawn a veiling mist drifts apart long enough to expose barren vistas as Kent and I stride into a 40-mile-long clearcut arena that rivals a demilitarized zone. The unconscionable scalping of every other hillside leaves me with a permanent brain scar, a sour stomach, and an urgent need for horse-blinders. The lush forest's natural harmony has been replaced by a patternless showcase of vulgarity. Blunt stumps and gouged bulldozer ruts abound. A few naked snags remain eerily silhouetted against the broad brown slope.

It is an unbelievably arrogant attitude that allows someone to destroy with machines something nature has nursed for centuries. In addition, these cumulative operations can permanently remove most of the soil's nutrients, and their replacement at altitude is painstakingly slow.

Kent virtually simulates a liquid-carrying pack mule in order to ward off possible dehydration as there is no water on or near the trail for 25 miles. He graciously insists on carrying most of our water because of the number of days I have been and will be out here.

Endless detours around logging areas force us to cover a great deal of extra mileage. Unfortunately, after being funneled out of the cutting area little effort is made to guide us back to the Pacific Crest Trail.

Two more veteran 100-mile trail runners, Russ Melanson and Carlos Arellanes (my first-summer sidekicks from Mammoth to Yosemite) run toward us from Stampede Pass, which averages over 250 fogged-in days annually, over badly disheveled turf. Ann has preceded them by one hour on the same trail following her long vehicle shuttle.

We round a sharp bend and are greeted by Ann's unrestrained embraces and infectious grin. Seemingly only moments later, we hear and see the war whoops and excited gestures emitting from a jubilant Russ and Carlos.

At days end five spirited runners stride into Stampede Pass like an alien centipede to quench a cumulative thirst. An hour later, the selfless Holders reluctantly slip into their camper to begin the grind southward.

Kent was to reflect on the adventure for many months to come, and later shared his thoughts on the run and why he and Ann went to the trouble to join me:

"My philosophy is that doing worthwhile things ultimately makes life worthwhile. I wanted to become an integral part of Bob's historical first-time run of the Pacific Crest Trail. I've been able in my life to take pride in doing for others what I might not have achieved for myself.

It was an opportunity and excuse to visit new sections of the country I might otherwise have never seen. Witnessing the many moods of Mt. Rainier, for example, turned out to be an inspirational experience. It was heartening, to say the least, to find Bob still excited after well over 2,000 miles of pounding over wilderness turf.

The wanton destruction of the forest in the clearcut was upsetting, and the thought that the Forest Service would allow such indiscriminate raping was incredible to me. The condition of the trail was equally upsetting with its lack of restoration after the clearcutting and the overall lack of maintenance.

Despite those down moments, knowing that I was among others who share a respect for nature gave the journey more meaning. I was infused with feelings of the incomparable brotherhood of man and caring about the earth. These feelings combined to emulate the highest possible spiritual experience that I can achieve.

On another plane, I was impressed that the human body can adapt so well in an undertaking of this magnitude, given proper nutrition, care, and rest. I thought Bob handled both time and distance remarkably well and was amazed that he could remain in good spirits under such grueling daily rigors.

Ann was just as eager to get involved in Bob's run as I was and I believe she was equally fulfilled. We purposely selected the most difficult-to-access area knowing our 4WD vehicle would allow us to get in. As in many other times in our marriage, Ann proved to be the ultimate partner and a spectacular crew member."

Each time a support person (or team) left me I had mixed emotions. For a short while I would be overwhelmed by loneliness and fearful of the solo stint ahead. It never really got any easier to adjust. On the other hand, there was this feeling that since the journey was essentially my own, I was back where I was supposed to be. Although I really couldn't have pulled this entire run off on my own, I wondered what would have happened had I attempted to do so.

Then I thought about their feelings. It wasn't that I ever really doubted they'd come for any other reason than wanting to be there and for the spirit of the adventure. Most of my cohorts would have an uneasy look when they left me, as if they were feeling a little guilty about going back to their comfortable lives. After experiencing the dangers entailed in the run I think perhaps some of them might have wondered if they would ever see me again. Hence, the hearty, protracted good-bye sessions that invariably occurred.

11 The Golden Finale _____

To endure is greater than to dare; to tire out hostile fortune; to be daunted by no difficulty; to keep heart when all have lost it; to go through intrigue spotless; to forego even ambition when the end is gained — who can say this is not greatness?

— William Thackery

Bureaucratic Constipation

Day 136 - August 2.   Morning light sneaks up and Carlos shadows me through more destruction on the most hideous slice of landscape since Mexico. Eighteen miles of toilsome bushwhacking require eight-and-one-half hours. Thick, shoulder-high growth on both sides of the trail is intermeshed and must be pulled apart to permit passage. The overgrowth is dangerous due to the deep ruts underneath.

Seventy-two-year-old Johnny Olley, a concerned wilderness devotee who has written many letters to Congress geared toward improving trail maintenance, slips on wet grass near midday and falls 30 feet, breaking an ankle in the process. He had been hiking the Pacific Crest Trail south from Canada. Search and rescue workers power walk into Mirror Lake to transport him out by litter just as we come running in. We exchange trail philosophies. Johnny says he will return after this delay that could easily have been a major tragedy.

The area where he fell harbors hidden holes, loose rocks, and is the epitome of disrepair due to budget cutbacks that many have labeled "bureaucratic constipation." The once valuable Civilian Conservation Corps, whose trained young crews manicured the Pacific Crest Trail in the past, has diminished in numbers and productivity. Today, huge stretches remain neglected resulting in jungle-thick brush that obscures sheer drop-offs.

While taking a breather for munchies and liquid, I search out a flat log to stretch out on. Behind it lies a tiny, quivering fawn, still slightly wet from its recent birth. Huddled in an almost fetal position like a ball of mottled, spotted fur, it is sleepy-eyed and nearly motionless except for visible fright.

A quiet chill of excitement moves up my spine. I try to be discrete with my quick stares, gazing only as long as I dare. Its outsized ears lay back flat against its neck. The spots on its back are aligned symmetrically, an off-white, perfectly blended into a background of milk chocolate brown. Twice it cocks its head for signs of danger. I could barely distinguish several sighs and soft grunts before it curls up and goes back to sleep.

Sleepy-eyed newborn fawn   by Mike Dirham

A fawn can stand within 15 minutes after being born, but takes about five times longer than that to walk. Nature gives it several days without any scent in order to gain strength enough to flee a predator.

I move on to hook up with Carlos, who has been ahead of me for some time, to share this privileged moment. Humans wish to be in control of the world. Animals just want to play a part.

Russ mountain bikes toward us. Recent toe surgery has curtailed his running. He pauses periodically to place inspirational notes, on small white cards, along our route. He either affixes them to Pacific Crest Trail posts or positions them with high visibility beside large rocks. Some say:

"Only two-and-one-half weeks to go."
"Stay mentally tough."
"You can do it."

Carlos and I press on.

Plaintive, stately elk move with awesome precision across a hillside laden with food. Several munch selectively on brush shoots, plant buds, and small branch tips.

We observe huge mushrooms, wild berries, drippy moss, miniature frogs, and magnificent floral festoons as we battle our way through a virtual sea of frustrating debris. A socked-in Snoqualmie Pass, the southern border of the North Cascades, is barely visible in the distance as billowing fog fills my pores with chill.

We encounter two long-term hikers with giant packs, wearing soaked ponchos and gaiters from an afternoon storm. They have gray hair, strong legs, and are headed south. We are able to swap war stories on trail conditions, bad stream crossings, and icy traverses. It seems nearly everyone I meet is at his or her ultimate level of contagious generosity. I am feeling loneliness creep in as Russ reserves a campsite, cooks two fantastic meals, then leaves with Carlos to drive 1,200 miles south the next morning.

Days 137-138 - August 3-4. Life-long friend and Washington resident, Amie Beisel, plucks my subdued frame from a picnic table bench and ushers me off to her nearby family retreat for a rest day. Lary Webster will match this selfless assistance tomorrow with a similar respite. I tingle with excitement waiting for the night to pass so that I might launch my refreshed spirit into a new day.

I often think, how can I actually look forward to more of this punishment? Am I ruining my body for life? What is holding me together? Perhaps because I know the end is near I can muster the necessary final motivation. I wonder whether there's a part of me, the flip side of never wanting to leave this surreal beauty, that longs for the familiar comfort of my little cottage by the sea. As the days pass I become more and more anxious about my upcoming reacclimation. How, for instance, will my friendships feel in light of this journey? Will I be so altered that there's no longer a common platform for communication? Perhaps it is wiser not to anticipate for I am in God's hands now. My fate will be determined by his will.

I dedicate this final sojourn to Ron Flowers, a cherished running companion. He died recently from Lou Gehrig's Disease, a malady that renders the muscles incapable of stabilizing the vital organs. We were preparing to embark on our premiere trail race together when he contracted this horrible ailment. He was slightly younger than me and a great friend. I dedicated my first 100-mile race to him. I mailed my award plaque to him with a personal inscription. It coincidentally arrived on his birthday. He sent an eloquent thank you note, typed because he could no longer grip a pen to write.

A 1,200-mile drive north brings iron-willed Lee Freeman, my Seiad Valley and Hyatt Lake second-summer partner to pace me throughout the majestic Alpine Lakes Wilderness. Before Lee departs at Stevens Pass he will have paced me for five days in three states.

Cascade Runoff

Day 139 - August 5.   The freckling rays of sunrise guide us as we weave along scree-strewn Chikamin Ridge. Lee and I then drop 2,000 feet from Park Lakes Basin to the thigh-high ford of Lemah Creek. I bathe in a secluded pool during a snack break. The cold water over my shoulders makes me shudder as a light breeze whips around my ears. I seem to be overdosed on clean air and surrounding scents under a flawless blue sky.

The day turns into a scorcher; dead still, no wind. The sweat falls from us in sheets. To much wind is like the enemy until there is none to cool your heated body; a moderate breeze is like a special friend arriving unexpectedly. We hastily add a thorough layer of sunscreen to ward off "old sol's" damaging rays.

The trail now traverses a field of glacial tarns dotted with ponds. A gently sloping valley opens up before us. On the horizon several lakelets radiate under the sun's golden light.

Day's end finds Lee and I replenishing ourselves with a simple fireside meal at tiny Pete Lake, under a wild sky literally ablaze with light shows. We feel like giddy youngsters as we sit on a flat boulder on the edge of a meadow and watch the stars, energized by each constellation's unveiling.

Day 140 - August 6.   A lower elevation alternate, semi-abandoned segment of the Pacific Crest Trail offers trailside streams. In the morning Lee and I follow this somewhat-butchered ribbon toward the soft beauty of slender, mirrored Waptus Lake where we replenish our water supply.

The main trail now tests our innermost grit as we throttle up Cathedral Pass with resiliency. Our knees melt into putty after running across rocks that range in size from golf balls to cantaloupes.

Our greatest hazard in Washington is the torrential streams, swollen during peak runoff, that must be crossed. We get mighty apprehensive when we battle a 25-mile-per-hour current over an unreliable, uneven streambed.

The worst currents have decibel levels of a runaway freight train, and as we wind down ragged ravines, we witness the water's explosive outbursts. The volume and speed of these turbulent mudbaths increase as the heat of the sun increases the snowmelt. Unfortunately we don't always arrive at the ideal time to cross.

Anticipating a hazardous ford, we, two wilderness ambassadors, now grunt with unchained resolve down the brown pathway. Just around the next bend as we run toward Deception Pass and below glacier-laden Mt. Daniel is the Pacific Crest Trail's most dangerous river crossing. We had hoped to cross the stream early in the day when the flow is low and slow,

Sorting gear by lean-to   by Willard Krick

but unexpected delays forced us well into the afternoon. Still we ignored the warning signs a few miles back that offered an alternate route.

The short hairs along my spine stand on end. I think about a conversation a week ago when a park ranger reiterated that the number one cause of wilderness fatalities in Washington is drowning. My heart pumps vigorously even though I am as well conditioned as I may ever be. Both legs quiver uncontrollably when I listen to the clamoring torrent.

Both my quads start to seize up on the lengthy descent to the stream. The medialis muscle in one quad decides to announce the presence of additional trauma, thus slowing me to a walk until I knead it out. After I finally succeed, the inner thigh muscle in the other quad sharply cramps and stays that way until I stop, rest, and stretch. I splash some icy stream water over my painful muscles and blurt out agonizing yips. Finally the stabbing sensation subsides.

We maneuver our rubbery lower appendages over flat rocks and moss-covered logs. Mercifully, a low snow year and slower currents enable a wet but upright passage across this brutal waterway.

After crossing we fortify ourselves with high energy bars, gorp, ibuprofen, and icy stream soaks. Fatigued, we spend tonight on a flat

Glacier Peak Wilderness   by Willard Krick

sandbar that bisects the two Deception Lakes, a pair of boulder-studded jewels. Undersides of the gray clouds that overlook us pick up the softest tints of pink.

Day 141 - August 7. An exhilarating dip in a large pond will climax today's 25-mile slice of grand and remote land.

Today we ambulate down to Stevens Pass. The trail resembles a verdant washboard. We pause and squint at Trap and Josephine lakes with their sparkling surface reflections etching our memory banks. Motionless mountain air enshrouds the near perfect landscape.

We have run by some 35 lakes in three days. I've run so far my personal odometer is almost inoperable. I feel like a human "Canadian Express" chugging toward an evasive terminal that always seems just out of reach.

I thank God that I have been blessed with the personal privilege of covering great distances with disciplined footstrikes. I am not the same person who began this run through these lovely, rugged mountains. I am overwhelmed by the depth and joy of what I have seen, heard, felt, and suffered.

I look back to my summer employee days of pumping gas for harried tourists in Yosemite who were barely able to get out of their self-imposed metal-and-chrome prisons. I will wager that 90 percent of their memories were filtered through a chipped, moving windshield. I chuckle at the incredible contrast between the superficial tourist traveling and my own journey. I feel so lucky to have been inwardly guided into this lifestyle of clean, hard effort, and its rewards.

On the trail ahead of me, rotund yellow-bellied marmots, the size of tiny blimps, sun worship on slab lookouts while eyeing me askance. These furry cavern dwellers whistle an astoundingly shrill warning to their comrades when humans or predators approach.

Coming toward us now is Washington runner John Middleton, the same superlative ultra athlete who supported me in California's High Sierra in 1985. He dodges a network of ski lifts and powerlines to applaud our trailhead approach. We shake out sore limbs en route to an upcoming fuel replacement.

Days 142-143 - August 8-9. On the first of two rest days, Lee departs at 4:30 a.m. to drive south to return to work. My friendship with this man has reached new heights. Lee's endurance and unselfishness will earn him a badge of honor in some other time frame. Besides being a caring and sensitive man, Lee is blessed with artistic talent as a photographer. His photographs of this spectacular rugged journey are some of the finest anywhere. He proves one incredible backcountry aficionado.

Looking northward, I notice subtle weather patterns and jumbles of fractured switchbacks. Starting tomorrow, I face over 10,000 feet of daily elevation change. Three of the next five days will entail over 28 miles each. Friends will bring in fresh shoes soon and I will need them. I consider the selfless assistance I have been given. I must have a guardian angel standing by at each new turn in the trail.

Running friend Willard Krick drives up from El Segundo in Southern California. He broke away from a family vacation trip to pace me on a two-day, 48-mile tenacity tester through a perennially wet segment of the Northern Cascades.

Another friend, Tim Lauridson, who cached water for me during summer one, also joins us. He is trim, fit, and a fast hiker.

Day 144 - August 10. Sap rises and life stirs. Inner juices ebb and flow, as stark shadows surround Willard and me. We are mentally ready. Tim has started walking two hours earlier. A passing pickup truck passenger chortles and guffaws at our skimpy outfits as we stretch out tight muscles in thick fog before starting out. Today's 28-mile run will include a ponderous haul around mist-veiled Grizzly Peak, a broad, exposed ridge laden with stunted pines and browning grasses.

We climb 3,000 feet to misty Lake Valhalla. Upon our arrival we spend many muddled minutes deciphering the correct trail. We're disoriented once more at Lake Janus due to unsigned junctions.

During the following five miles we pass by three lakes that we cannot see because of low-lying, dense clouds. These clouds will stay with us all the way to the top of 5,597-foot Grizzly Peak. The three of us encounter a temporary roadblock; a crew is dynamiting the trail above Pear Lake. Since Willard, Tim, and I often travel at different speeds we use this opportunity to regroup and snack in a nearby meadow.

Tim, restless from walking, decides to run with Willard and me throughout the next segment. He soon develops serious blisters from the continuous hammering down a long series of steep hills in stiff hiking boots.

The brush and flowers stand shoulder high at times. The trail is narrow with vertical drop-offs up to 800 feet.

We plummet downward to Cady Creek, refill our water bottles, and then grind out the ascent to Cady Pass. A late afternoon wind proves soul-chilling cold and numbs my appendages, especially my fingertips. Three fingers immediately turn milky white, drained of all their normal color.

Lake Sally Ann is 50 feet away before we see it at dusk. It has taken us eleven-and-a-half hours, including lunch stops, hiker visits, and map scrutiny, to find our way on the Pacific Crest Trail today.

A large snowbank serves as our nocturnal backdrop. Our white socks are black. Our running shoes are wearing thick mud overcoats. Jagged small rocks and splintered wood chips decorate their insides.

Willard and I pray for warmer temperatures as we sit under our tarp. A tiny fire is not generating much warmth due to wet wood. Tim walks in by flashlight at 9:00 p.m.

After we are all fed and settled in, a large mouse crawls onto our ground cover to nibble tidbits of spilled granola only inches from our heads. After a half dozen more visits it finally runs off gorged.

The ground is rock-hard, so our hip bones take a pretty good thrashing. Willard bellows in pain with calf cramps during the night. Just before dawn he gets chilled and starts shivering. My snoring encourages his insomnia.

It is so cold that delicate ice crystals etch the surrounding leaves and needles that line our makeshift bedroom. A frozen mist filters through the dripping natural screen of dense fir.

Day 145 - August 11. The fog and our own borderline doldrums disappear by midmorning. Our vision is clear. Glacier Peak and Mt. Rainier face each other and act as guiding beacons. Rainier serves as a mountain climber's mecca and hiking paradise to hardy, fit Washingtonians. Its dominating presence and spectacular beauty elicit immense pride amongst the people in this state. Twenty mountain peaks, some with massive glaciers, assert themselves with an awesome alpine authority. 10,541-foot Glacier Peak has four separate glaciers alone.

A profusion of flowers sweep up the hillsides from living mountain meadows and lace the air with fragrant smells. Nearby, elk and deer roam across grassy slopes, some the size of ten football fields. Soft multiple hues of rich green and brown bathe the terrain and are quite a contrast to the earlier rainforest-like mist. Intermittent clouds emerge to drain color from the landscape. I feel like an ant in an immense land.

We are almost able to pet two marmots in a secluded grotto at 6,500-foot Red Pass as mottled shafts of sunlight angle through the clouds. Both marmots resemble chamois-colored, elongated, horsehair pillows as they lie motionless, half buried in windblown debris.

Clusters of tiny blue butterflies cling to the trail which bisects a lengthy alpine meadow. I could even hear the soft flick of something fluttering over the low brush.

We descend 3,000 feet in the next seven miles; some of it steep. We follow the White Chuck River which crashes heavily down the mountainside over bladed rock. We cross the river myriad times on bridges, logs, and precarious rock fords. The stream gathers force each time it picks up a new tributary, charging and toppling over waist-high cascades into tempting pools with ominous eddies.

On a bridge we hear the roar of a massive waterfall. The raging water, augmented by two 25-foot drops, churns upward from the chalky-tinted turbulence below. Not far beyond, the thick silt-laden flows of White Chuck and Kennedy Creeks converge in frothing, foaming fury.

Tim hikes on alone while Willard and I embark on a two-mile, side trail pilgrimage to soothing 96-degree Kennedy Hot Spring. A piped spring, jutting out among small, primitive stands of firs, provides pure drinking water that doesn't require treating. Hypnotically, we immerse our tortured torsos in a five-foot deep, rock-lined natural hot tub that murmurs softly with intermittent bubbles.

A well-deserved soak at Kennedy Hot Spring   by Willard Krick

A bivysack "sponge"   by Mike Dirham

Our elevation change these last two days has exceeded 20,000 feet and Willard is not done.

After the hot soak, Willard runs toward a nearby trailhead. About halfway, he meets his wife, Jean, and two close friends, Chuck and Nancy Giardini. They are hiking in with my food cache and fresh shoes.

Willard shoves both items into his daypack, runs back to the hot spring, then carries my worn shoes out. He reaches civilization well after 10 p.m. This is one special human being.

The adventure stayed with Willard for some time, and he felt the need to share his own feelings and fears:

"I knew I was into something big when we met a woman hiker from British Columbia who walked up and said,

'Oh, you're the runners going to Canada.' She'd heard it from other hikers 200 miles south.

On my first day of punishing climbs and descents I understood how much it took for Bob to do that day after day after day. The biggest obstacle was the constant struggle just to stay on the trail, followed by the cliff-edged drops that got my heart pounding every time we encountered them. And when the cold became debilitating I could only imagine how long some of those nights had been for Bob. After a night of pulsating, cramping quadriceps, the thought of doing it all over again was less than pleasant.

All in all, I found I needed to do just what Bob had done — transcend the pain and discomfort in order to take in the beauty all around me."

Terra Firma is Steep and Mud is Deep

Day 146 - August 12. Alone again. Nothing is as important as today and nothing is as uncertain as tomorrow. A dawn rain hammers that lesson resoundingly home; it is the beginning of 18 hours of body-blanching precipitation. Violent rain turns rockhard ground into slick mud. Chipmunks arise from hidden nests for fear they might drown. Thirsty, gregarious mosquitoes seemingly receive an "all-points" bulletin stating the date and location of their annual convention. It is here and now!

That evening the air temperature plummets below 40 degrees as the unrelenting downpour cuts through dense fog on 30-mph winds. I slide downslope five feet while still huddled in a somewhat fetal position and zipped inside my bivy. Hailstones sledgehammer evenly spaced impressions on my head and neck. I am a prone prisoner in a saturated ultralight Gore-Tex cocoon. I sneak a peak at the overwhelming elements that threaten to permeate the paper-thin walls of my wilderness home.

I purposely roll 35 yards to a thudding halt underneath two intertwined tree canopies. Chattering teeth bite through my lower lip. My brain is on idle.

Day 147 - August 13. I stagger out to meet the world sometime around 8 a.m. I roll, band, and strap-on my wet gear. Firewood is sparse and very wet. It's time to move on before I look any more like a sponge in a monsoon.

Wonderful John Middleton from Everett, Washington bounds in from a roadside trailhead to shadow me for 48 hours. His tenure on this soaked mountain tread will not be blessed with a single ray of sunlight. With white-knuckled numbness and squishing shoes we hunch our shoulders and lean into the onslaught.

Noisy rain pellets driven by the wind at our backs push us deep into the wilderness and up a 3,100-foot haul to Fire Creek Pass. We immediately drop 2,500 feet to turbulent Milk Creek where finger-sized banana slugs writhe in the muck and mire.

Shoulder-high vegetation, thick with festoons of wildflowers, impedes us on another 2,200-foot backbusting upswing to a scree-covered plain. A multi-switchbacked, 3,200-foot downgrade to Vista Creek completes this masochistic section. Chilling, incessant fog envelops us as we pass through twisted firs.

By wearing the right combination of polypropylene and Gore-Tex, ingesting a PowerBar and trail mix "double whammy" for the fuel tank, while making minimal stops, we manage to keep our body temperature up.

At no time do I ever feel underdressed, depressed, or on the verge of a major bailout. Today's uncertainties and anxieties will soon be history if we have ample patience. I never consider any other option. Throughout I feel it is important to keep a positive focus on the excitement that hard-earned achievement brings. I dream of conquering the border up ahead. By now I have developed the serenity of a Zen master.

John and I experience incredibly dense sections of trees in Washington with nary a viewpoint. Map and compass skills become crucial in this alien landscape often blanketed with large snowfields or thick fog.

It is discouraging to lose several thousand feet of elevation gain we just sweated blood for, then face a repeat performance of climbing and descending several times over.

Discomfort from sore feet is now compounded by a steepening trail, deep holes, and sections chiseled by erosion.

At the iron-stained Seattle River bridge we reel in Tim Lauridsen who has been hiking one day ahead.

That evening, thick, stinging smoke emanates from the damp bark of our fire. A light drizzle stimulates a profound hissing amongst the burning coals and creates tiny puffs of soot and steam. I am scorched on the front while intimately stroking the fire, yet bone-chilled in the rear by the relentless wind. Soon the aroma of burning wood is replaced by the stench of burning polypropylene and rubber. In our eagerness to dry out in the mist we thoroughly singe our shirt sleeves, sock tops, and shoes.

The rain expresses its seeming displeasure by venting with an all-night drum roll on our tiny tarp lean-to. There are no stars or moon as howling winds toss and whip the wetness.

I thrust numb appendages into my crotch and armpits for warmth. I prepared for this weather; I expect it. But I don't have to like it. Although there are only ten days left until I carry my weary body across the border, I am praying they won't be as nasty as this one.

This symphony of subtle pain plays skillfully with my nerves. Weathering this temporary agony transcends my weaknesses and proves I'm still in control. What's more, it could be snowing in August (not uncommon

Ahh! The smell of burning rubber   by Mike Dirham

here), and I am blessed with warm clothes and good friends. I am determined to savor, not rush, these remaining days.

Day 148 - August 14. With a new dawn's wet-but-smoldering wood
fire nearly out, three intrepid hombres get mentally ready for a repeat
enduro. John, Tim, and I ramble philosophically while the last coals tinkle.
We share a few tall tales.

John leads, Tim handles the rear, and I run between them on a tenacious 30-miler. A startled marmot darts tail up through my legs and
disappears after a full-speed waddle.

The trail catapults us up, then down a wildly-cloven valley through
emerald forests splashed with ferns. Stones polished like rubbed silver
echo the water cascading down Agnes Creek.

A raven circles in a thermal high above. It tucks and dives like a
cardboard airplane breaking with authority at the last minute. A covey of
small grouse scutter off into the underbrush. A gravel-throated gray squirrel complains of my intrusion from his high perch as glinting light showcases cloud-like glaciers across a web of sharply etched peaks. The sweetness
of the surroundings lubricates my mind. Cerebral pathways are clicking.

With all the endorphins swimming around I can't suppress a wide grin. While mountain running has vastly increased my patience, it has also done wonders for my sense of humor.

After ten hours to High Bridge Guard Station, we run five more bedraggled miles to a prearranged stop at a Stehekin cabin on the northern edge of 46-mile-long, fiord-like Lake Chelan. The rain finally subsides. Sporadic bouts of lightning flicker in the vibrant summer evening.

Party Hearty

Day 149-152 - August 15-18.   At dawn a multi-hued rainbow high above the Stehekin River stimulates my imagination. My tastebuds, so long ignored, now stir in anticipation of "real" food — anything other than gorp, rice cakes, and granola.

A four-hour Lake Chelan boat cruise takes us to the Lauridsen ranch in Manson where Tim's family bathes us three nomads in cloistered warmth.

On the final rest day, I return to Stehekin by seaplane. John and Tim depart southward from the ranch.

I have now completed 106 wilderness running days. My contentment at this moment is supreme. I refrain from getting cocky for I know I am not yet there. I may well face a worse storm.

I almost feel a need to apologize for the decadent living of the past two days: sunbathing motionless on a boat dock, sauntering (with a full stomach) through apple orchards without a wet, throbbing fanny pack, and now flying over the outskirts of the very land I have just traversed by foot. It feels unreal. I am shocked when I suddenly contemplate that I have only four running days left until, God willing, I reach that magic monument, the Canadian border. Life is sweet.

Stehekin is a charming hamlet snugly shoehorned into the northern channel of a narrow glacial chasm. Its population is a few hundred at the most, and it is accessible only by foot, boat or seaplane. Supplies are brought in by boat infrequently in amounts to last for several months. The few automobiles and pickup trucks look like they have spent a decade in a demolition derby. The only road they can really travel is 23 miles long and dead-ends in both directions.

Stehekin is an Indian term for "pass through." The irony is amusing. Although Stehekin was on a major trade route in the Cascades decades ago, it is really off the beaten track now. The area's earliest inhabitants, the Indians, spoke with reverence of Mother Earth, of taking her openly proffered fruits, and not scratching her surface with machines. These people attempted to mesh with nature, not dominate her. They actually lived in such a way as to adapt themselves to the environment, not change it to suit their needs.

The Indians had a simple philosophy and respect for all of the earth's inhabitants. They would leave no trace of passage over the land. One legend says that the Indians here would actually ask each berry if it was ready to leave its "mother" bush before they would pluck it.

Some of the Indians were runners, treading lightly and disturbing nothing with their lithe movements. I suspect they would often stop and listen for the silent treasures of total quiet. Constant ringing in the ears from city living would doubtless have confounded them. I like to think they might have been the very first wilderness runners and that, as such, I have a kinship with them. They once considered it a disgrace to die in bed, and I guess I feel the same way.

I visit with Stehekin ranger Mardell Gunn who has walked the entire trail. An all-you-can-eat bunkhouse meal by a roaring fire at nearby Courtney Ranch ignites my inner juices for tomorrow's miles.

Animal Traffic and Precarious Ledges

Day 153 - August 19. Daybreak kicks in and I run north out of High Bridge Campground. A foul-smelling wolverine dashes across the path on short, stout legs, his belly almost touching the ground. His hair plumes out on all sides as he scampers into a sprawling thicket. The wolverine has a reputation for being, pound for pound, one of the meanest animals in the forest. Also, it is rarely visible and I feel privileged to actually see one.

Moments later I startle a burly black bear and observe its clamorous flight pattern as it thunders with abandon down a gnarled gradient. By now I have developed the vigilance of a guard dog. Flashing through my mind is a fleeting, though vivid, picture of vise-like bear jaws clamping deep into the flesh of my thigh, grinding to the bone.

I quickly tune it out as I meet up with a backcountry ranger, cleaning firepits, with whom I chat and share a wild huckleberry snack.

I pass some off-trail forest hide-a-ways, then nearly collide with my next companion, 747 pilot and ultra trail runner Court Mumford. He has been striding toward me from Rainy Pass. Our friendship is deep since that wet and frightening final day in Oregon. We share our memories throughout a glorious afternoon romp.

We arrive at the campground at Rainy Pass where an excited Janis Mumford breaks out a sumptuous pasta dish. I sign an autograph for a paraplegic athlete who was working out on a specially designed wheelchair path nearby. Court, Janis, and I recline under a starlit sky.

Day 154 - August 20. We are up at 5:30 a.m. for coffee and oatmeal. Today's 31-miler will include ten hours of rigorous, cliff-edge running, interspersed with carefree floating through thick woods on brown needles. As human vessels we become intensely involved in our surroundings, feeling a part of them after running only a few moments.

A tiny flashlight falls out of my hat while shedding upper layers of clothing so I can soak in the much welcomed sun in this gorgeous paradise.

I had hurriedly shoved it in there during the early morning start. My running cap was pulled down tightly and I didn't feel the flashlight's weight or movement.

I am beginning to mentally space out after the cumulative fatigue of trail running. On especially arduous days, around dusk I find my subconscious manufacturing hallucinations of massive bears under swaying firs. But today I have no excuse; it is only 10 a.m.

Descriptive trailside signs have been motivating me throughout the journey, but today's is fitting:

> There are no strangers on the trail, only friends you haven't met yet.

Another pleads eloquently:

> Take care of the land. Some day you'll be part of it.

One wooden sign articulates former Secretary of the Interior Stewart Udall's ability to see beyond the obvious:

> Bigger may not be better, slower may be faster, less may well mean more.

In some areas, saboteurs have obliterated trail posts in a vengeful defiance as though the presence of a national trail threatens their mechanized operations.

Before loggers clearcut they are required to build a temporary trail detour around their operations. They may resent the time it takes to do this. Vengefully they sometimes destroy the signs that mark the main trail.

There are no trail markers today, only a few battered signs as we sidestep huge stacks of steaming packhorse scat indicating civilization and tonight's camp are not far away.

Jack Slater will be my shadow for the final two days (32 miles) to Canada. An outstanding ultrarunner from Southern California, Jack culminates a three-state, 1,300-mile drive by striding out to meet us on a rugged ridgeline near Harts Pass. Jack has been runner-up champion at the Angeles Crest 100-Miler. He is a tenacious trail race competitor as well as a fantastic person.

Court and I now sight Jack coming toward us. Now we run as a trio toward an ecstatic Janis, who has driven around by road to meet us.

At Harts Pass, I regretfully say good-bye to the incredible Mumfords and consider that we'll probably never unite again under the exact same circumstances.

Hans Holtz, Jack's hometown motoring companion, will transport some of our dunnage to Canada. Washington ultradistance runner Jim

Successful completion of another day   by Willard Krick

Taylor will bring several members of his running club over 100 miles by car to pace us across the border. The relentless and dependable John Middleton will bump his way toward the terminus of my journey on fire roads via mountain bike in order to greet us.

At this point it seems more like a party than a solitary journey, but I accept it with the thought that many wilderness guides recommend traveling in groups through this part of the Cascades. Ideally you should have three people: one to go for help and one to stay with the injured person if trouble strikes. Because of my support I was able to carry less weight in this final section of the trail.

I am amazed when I think of all the people who volunteered to help me through this critical segment. They say they are here to be a part of history, but there are no guarantees. They're here because they're unselfish; that's the bottom line. After running all of California and Oregon nearly 70-percent solo, I have been blessed with a fit companion almost every day in Washington. No matter whether the support person came for three days or three hours, I made sure I mailed them a personal progress report on rest days.

The farther I progressed north the greater the danger. This area can be unsafe for an isolated runner with light gear on unprotected ridges. Even though my own extensive map ability sometimes permitted me greater trail savvy than those with me, it was safety I prayed for and company I craved.

My friends ran with me as pacers and delivered crucial food parcels carried to me on their hipbelts or driven in across primitive routes. I owe them all a lifetime of gratitude. They gave meaning to my life during some of the roughest times, and encouraged my persistence and determination to continue.

We had good talks during hard times, creating a bridge of temporary comfort. This interaction made us feel good about ourselves and what we were doing. Without the shared risk there would be no success or failure. I suspect we all grapple continuously for a handle on a purpose larger than ourselves.

Reaching Sight of the Barn

Day 155 - August 21. With gear ratios set on high, adrenalin pumping, and great weather, Jack and I set out to make these final miles truly memorable.

We drift over seven passes to Hopkins Lake. A pair of jays squawk incessantly at each other, leapfrogging from tree to tree in the dappled greenery. Rich smells ooze from the blur of wildflowers blanketing the damp earth, and poison oak and beargrass compete for space.

The older I get the less appeal there is to traditional racing. An ugly, congested road shoulder ultimately becomes boring. After I had achieved time-structured goals, personal records became a lesser priority. I shed that tunnel vision and start slowing down long enough to look at the many things I had missed due to self-imposed competitive rushing.

On this three-summer trail run I have been able to absorb each detail, stopping as often as I wish because I've built in time to stop. I couldn't list the many incomparable moments or describe fully the rewards of cementing lifetime bonds with the people who came along for some part of my journey. I never cease to be awestruck by the friendships with complete strangers.

As we approach the Hopkins Lake basin I pump both arms vigorously hoping my legs will follow. We scramble downgrade which puts limits on our speed and forces ungraceful locomotion over highly corrugated tread.

Hopkins Lake is a small jewel nestled in a mountain bowl. Tiny flashes of sunlight shimmer on the lake surface. These enticing reflections welcome us into camp.

A crackling fire serves as center stage for the final trail mix and energy bar meal. The audible snapping and popping fills me with a melodic warmth. I feel a rustic self-sufficiency and a lively inner peace. The fragrant aroma of burning wood is a good companion.

Four fallow deer spend part of the evening with us. Two of them caper with playful leaps and awkward stumbling turns, then finally tumble into a heap, culminating an unrehearsed yet entertaining performance.

The Last Day

Day 156 - August 22. The early light floods over the smells welling up from a soft green meadow. I feel a part of this land. The trees seem to grow taller in this narrowing valley. I am so excited on this final running day that I feel as if I'm virtually gliding over the trail. Propelled by a fairly strong tailwind I practically race the sun. My body sings in harmony with the challenging terrain. I find myself daydreaming at mirrored ponds.

We now blaze downhill along neat rows of copper-sheened tree bark toward Monument 78 and the international border. I run red-eyed and numb with disbelief. The tears begin to well as I reach deep into my soul for a clue as to what I'm really feeling. My spiritual strength has grown out of a physical endurance that extended beyond normal boundaries. My very survival has relied upon the fused chemistry of mental discipline and persistent stamina.

That once wide span between fantasy and reality funnels down to a solidly connected web. Sporting black toes and dirt-caked fingernails I grin from ear to ear through my whiskered, grubby face. The corners of my lips and my heel bottoms are raw and cracked. I look like I have a trail runner's version of hoof-and-mouth disease.

It is day 156 and I have just crossed over onto Canadian soil paced by my guardian angel, Jack Slater, and the four Washington trail runners led by Jim Taylor. John Middleton cruises in as our sole greeter just as we arrive. We celebrate with PowerBars, a swig of Bodyfuel, some dried fruit, and sign the monument register. Hans shuttles the car around and will meet us at Manning Park (seven miles away) for a huge celebration.

We are so fired up that we sprint those seven miles. It takes all the concentration I can muster to comprehend this moment. Covering 2,581 miles in 22 weeks I have averaged 118 miles of running per week, mostly at oxygen-poor altitudes on rough, rocky footing.

I take a quiet moment to contemplate the staggering emotional impact of running so unencumbered for all those days.

Though many of my previous runs were entirely solo, wilderness running elicits a natural camaraderie, and I often found myself surrounded by friends, other runners, and interested spectators. "Aloneness" is not really alone. On this trip my idea of alone changed. Some days I ached so acutely for companionship that my stomach knotted and I became startled by my own breathing. Most of the time, though, aloneness was exhilarating. Knowing that I could yell from a mountaintop, and no human being

The sweet touch and feel of Canadian soil at Monument 78   by Jack Slater

would hear me, thrilled me over and over. It elicited a feeling I will never forget.

I ultimately became a most discriminating listener. The frolicking hillside dashes of friendly mule deer, the scream of a nesting black hawk, the shrill warning whistle of a marmot, the mournful howl of an owl were like invitations to their worlds — simple and beautiful havens from life's stresses. To put it simply, I was just very grateful they would let me in.

Ever on the watch for creatures who might not be so friendly, I gained a personal understanding of the brute strength and power of the larger beasts. A single elk only a few yards away could shake the entire mountaintop and cause me to lose footing on the trail beneath me. A sleek mountain cat could whip through the woods and simultaneously cause my body hair to stand on end and pull an involuntary gasp from my throat.

It is well known that crisis, loneliness, or proximity can bond mere acquaintances in a very short time. Many of the people I met on the trail greeted me like a long lost friend. Though our destinations and modes of traveling differed, it was as if the wilderness itself selected us to be honored recipients of its cumulative pleasures and promises. Several encounters would move me to tears; yet afterward I had no clear sense of why I was crying.

At times I found that I was transported by more than my aching limbs. The wilderness lent me its strength. Its hugeness and my smallness humbled me. As my universe expanded to match that around me, it appeared that I had more and more entities to thank each night for my safe passage. With nothing but the treetops between me and the stars, I felt that anything I had to do the next day would be possible. I'd see a splotch of nature, like a 360-degree vista from a jagged, high-country spine, and it would make me consider myself a mere speck in an expanding universe. All of this touched me with a lasting, spiritually nourishing perspective on who I am and why I'm here.

Throughout the journey there were huge sections of the trail that were poorly marked and grossly neglected. Many signs had incorrect mileages. And yet it is still a fantastic trail. The hardest moments could be grouped into two general categories: times when I was scared, and times when I was tired and/or sore and/or wet. The scary ones were usually associated with snow; crossing high altitude, steeply-pitched snow fields where I really did not want to slip, or below where the melted snow sometimes formed raging torrents. Crossing both the snow and the torrents caused me some extremely anxious moments. And then there were the times, particularly in the Northern Cascades, when the seemingly continuous rain combined with sore feet to test my own stores of patience, character, and tenacity.

The material trappings that accompany society were furthest from my mind, but I couldn't help but think how I could possibly tolerate future urban noise and density. Will my solitary mannerisms be suspect if I walk through my hometown wearing grubby trail clothes for the next year? Or will others sense the personal satisfaction that operates within my soul?

After overcoming the rigors of nearly 2,600 miles, no difficulty can be insurmountable tomorrow. But this is today and we're going to whoop it up!

Indelible Impressions

This has been the longest trail run in history, as well as the first time anyone has run across the United States in any direction by trail.

Miraculously I was toppled only three times in three summers — felled either by tiny hidden tree stumps or loose gravel on smooth rock. The water bottles would soften the surprise landings somewhat, and a knee cap or ribs might take the secondary impact. I have fallen more often each year in mountain runs near my home.

I leaped across or darted by more than 40 rattlesnakes. I surprised ten bears — fortunately all in the daytime. Enough bears for a lifetime.

In past years, I've slept next to friends whom bears have clumsily stepped on or brushed against while foraging for food in camp. I made up my mind early on never to encourage a late night theft by a bear because of personal negligence. A ripped or shredded hip pack could have meant disaster. I was also fortunate that the bears I did encounter were usually well fed at the moment — munching on berries near the trail.

In addition to nearly a thousand deer that frequented my nocturnal habitats or interrupted my daytime running, I spotted dozens of placidly grazing elk, three bighorn sheep, two wild goats, a wolverine, a couple of cougars, one bobcat, a golden eagle, wild turkey, coyotes, and a family of grouse right on the trail. The wildlife "standards" were the porcupines, squirrels, mice, countless species of birds, and nearly 75 shrieking marmots.

Some days every nerve ending tingled in anticipation of what might occur. Each night I borrowed no more space than a resting doe. Four-legged critters would crackle through thickets, frolicking within a cloud cover's perimeter, then blend into the chilling mountain mist. Tame chipmunks would rummage for gorp and granola crumbs, a thumb's width from my earlobe, under a nighttime sky. If I was reasonably alert, an aura of calm would enshroud a sluggish, unprovoked rattler, as it sauntered away with a characteristic tongue flick.

Daily sights, sounds, and smells came from streamside gurgling, fresh pine scents, breezes that cooled sweaty pores, whistling animal tirades, the flutter of startled birds, squeals from the squirrel kingdom, the thumping echoes of woodpeckers, or the pulsating coals from a tiny fire.

I was mentally geared to bypass a heavily snowbound section and return to run it when it was safe. Miraculously I was never behind schedule and twice I emerged a half-day early from the forested glades. Whenever "burnout" struck out at me, some new encounter or circumstance would turn my outlook around.

In 110 days I pounded every conceivable surface from shards of unforgiving volcanic rock to boggy quagmires in dense rainforest.

Cumulative elevation gain and descent has totaled close to one-half million feet of wild backcountry undulation.

After downing over 1,300 quarts of liquid on running days alone, I suspect I may have set a record in an event I never thought about competing in. Surprisingly I lost not an ounce of weight in any summer; maybe even gained a pound or so.

I sloshed along under precipitation an average of one in every six days in California and Oregon. This ratio doubled in Washington.

I sought, fought, and survived the intensity of a monumental task. Initially, I might have attacked its immensity to set myself apart. When I reached that sweet border I rejoiced in my new found love of the mountains, and a genuine affection for all the precious individuals who pitched in to get me there.

I learned to move in purposeful harmony while nurturing both restlessness and richness of passion.

I realize that I received a fair smattering of luck as though some higher force had "allowed" me safe transit. I could possess ultimate knowledge of the wild, prepare for a lifetime, and still be victimized by a major, irretractable mistake or by nature's ways. I adapted throughout an environmental puzzle without altering or destroying any piece.

Our most innate rewards stem from deep-seated, persistent struggle. I thought about my life, what I had done with it, and what I had yet to do. The unadulterated joy in mastering a test of such depth brought immense pride. When one wrestles with nature one feels a special thrill that cannot possibly be felt by those who make no effort. The wilderness has so much to give and gives it so openly that one yearns to return. It is highly motivating to challenge nature and difficult to dispel the fear of the unpredictable.

I developed a self reliance, conciseness, and efficiency, and learned the value of being humbled.

I cannot help but think my trail experiences are directly responsible for making me a better human being. The day-to-day struggle and its cumulative effects have intensified my directional priorities and purified my lifestyle.

I am driven now by the need to become a spiritual travel agent for others willing to stretch their bodies and minds in a similar venture. If I can help others to make a similar journey, traveling with only the bare necessities, their lives may gain order as mine has done. It will enrich them in a way that only less, not more, can.

I know this happens. Coming home I was taken aback to find that any task or goal, by comparison, seemed insignificant. I felt I could do almost anything with my eyes closed.

And that's the beauty of it. My senses, once touched by the ultimate sounds, sights, and smells of nature, are forever altered. And yet I feel no need to test this new found discovery. It is enough that I have been so blessed and changed.

Afterward

In truth, it doesn't matter what the journey is — running the Pacific Crest Trail or simply pitting yourself against nature for a week in your local mountains. The point is to plan to do it and then do it. If it represents the biggest thing you have ever done the effect will be the same. You will find it is well worth the effort making the leap between something envisioned and something done. And you'll wonder why you didn't do it sooner.

Those timid souls, who never extend beyond their self-imprisoning comfort levels, will never know their own capacities.

Physical limitations need not stop you. Consider Bob Barker. Although handicapped by multiple sclerosis he recently walked the Appalachian Trail from Georgia to Maine on crutches. Contemplate the mental toughness and courage of Bill Irwin, a 50-year-old recovering alcoholic. He hiked the same trail totally blind, aided only by his seeing-eye dog who followed the scents of previous foot travel. On some days Bill fell over 35 times.

Lastly, once you do it, put it in print so that others may share your adventure. It will be a gift of timeless value.

Epilogue

There is a right way and a wrong way to run great distances, just as there is to write at great length. People who think they know how such things work thought Bob Holtel went about both big jobs all wrong.

Experts on ultramarathoning said the border-to-border run couldn't — or at least shouldn't — be done as Bob planned it. Authorities in publishing said he couldn't or shouldn't write the book he planned.

The right way to run across the United States would be the west-east path taken by runners before or the shorter south-north route from Mexico to Canada while hugging the Pacific Coast. Either way, the course should pass through the major cities for maximum publicity.

He should find sponsors, and rent a motor home for himself and another for his support crew (it's most important member being a publicist to announce the run on network talk shows and arrange interviews at every stop along the way).

Bob ran his way, the hard way. He went out of his way to avoid the roads and the hoopla. He chose the remote Pacific Crest Trail over the crowded Pacific Coast Highway.

Bob wrote his book his way, in his own words. He forced them onto paper and then into print with the same will that carried him north from Mexico to Canada through the high country.

The fact that you've now read at this length about a three-summer trip proves that the "wrong" ways worked just right for a man used to taking the trails less traveled.

Joe Henderson
West Coast Editor for Runner's World[1]

---

[1] Organization given for identification only.

Gear

- Large Alpenlite nylon fanny pack (top zippered pocket converts to a daypack)

- Alpenlite Gore-Tex bivouac sack (space blanket-like material sewn inside and mosquito netting at the head)

- Recreational Equipment Inc. (REI) quilted, Texolite sleeping bag liner

- Small featherweight tarp with grommets and cords at each corner

- Two 24-ounce plastic water bottles with Bodyfuel mixed inside (occasionally one or more extra 16-ounce bottles)

- Two Bottle Totes (heavy duty Velcro bottle-holders)

- Clothes

    Three Patagonia Capilene shirts with V-neck zipper (one lightweight, one medium weight, and one expedition weight)

    One pair Patagonia featherweight Capilene pants

    Two pair nylon running shorts

    Two pair polypropylene socks

    One Patagonia quilted, polypropylene, hooded sweatshirt (also used as a rolled up wedge under fanny pack to facilitate snugness)

    One New Balance Gore-Tex lightweight rainsuit

    One Gore-Tex raincap (polypropylene-lined on inside with visor and earflaps)

    One lightweight Patagonia Capilene balaclava

    Two visored suncaps

    Polypropylene gloves and Gore-Tex outer shells

    One bandanna

    Two medium-size plastic bags for use as vapor barrier socks at night

    One pair New Balance running shoes (577s or 997s)

- Topographical maps for next several days stored in Ziploc plastic bag (for extreme compactness used those from *Pacific Crest Trail, Volumes I & II*, by Jeffrey Schaffer, et. al.)

- Compass

- Small Tekna flashlight plus extra batteries and bulb
- Lightweight knife
- Sunglasses with UV protection and cord-holder
- Waterproof and windproof matches in plastic container
- Gel-type fire starter
- Plastic whistle
- Tiny emergency space blanket stored in Ziploc plastic bag
- Tiny bottle of water purification tablets
- Toilet paper stored in Ziploc plastic bag
- Toothbrush with half-handle (no paste)
- Two plastic trash bag raincoats (also used to protect fanny pack or as a vapor barrier liner under shirt)
- Fine felt-tip pen and note pad in Ziploc plastic bag
- Savex lip ice
- Sunscreen (SPF 15)
- Skin lotion
- Mosquito repellent
- Two six-inch-square foam pads to prevent hip abrasion while running and for padding hip and shoulder at night
- Medical kit (courtesy of Dr. John Pagliano, past president of the American Academy of Podiatric Sports Medicine and one-time American record holder for 50 miles; and Dr. Bruce Letvin, my hometown podiatrist)

    Felt forefoot pads

    Spenco insoles

    Rubber heel pads

    Moleskin (pre-cut)

    Ankle brace (elastic, cloth sleeve type)

    Sponge separation pads for between big toe and second toe

    Antifungal foot cream

    Antifungal foot powder

    Tiny toe clippers

  Callus sander

  Sterile needle to drain blisters

  Durable Band-Aids

  Aspirin (coated) and Advil

  Lomotil tablets for diarrhea

  Flagyl tablets for giardia

  Medicated eye drops for bacterial infection and irritation

  Small plastic plunger and suction cup for snakebites

- Food for several days

  Bodyfuel (stored in tiny Ziploc plastic bags)

  PowerBars

  Mealpack bars

  Granola bars

  Date bars

  Trail mix (Gorp)

  Dried fruit (peaches, apples, bananas, raisins, apricots)

  Nuts

  Granola

  Rice cakes

  Turkey jerky

Weekly Summary

Summer of '85

Week	Dates	Start & End	Mileage	Run Days	Rest Days	Passes, Gaps, and Junctions
1	July 10 thru July 16	Mexican Border to Idyllwild	148	6	1	None
2	July 17 thru July 23	Idyllwild to Silverwood Lake	146 (294)[1]	5 (11)	2 (3)	San Gorgonio Pass - 1,188' Onyx Summit - 8,510'
3	July 24 thru July 30	Silverwood Lake to Messenger Flats Campground	102 (396)	6 (17)	1 (4)	Cajon Junction - 3,020' Vincent Gap - 6,585' Mill Creek Summit - 4,910'
4	July 31 thru Aug. 6	Messenger Flats Campground to Walker Pass	155 (551)	5 (22)	2 (6)	Bird Spring Pass - 5,355' Walker Pass - 5,246'
5	Aug. 7 thru Aug. 13	Walker Pass to Horseshoe Meadow[2]	97 (648)	5 (27)	2 (8)	Mulkey Pass - 10,380' Trail Pass - 10,500' Cottonwood Pass - 11,160'
6	Aug. 14 thru Aug. 20	Horseshoe Meadow to Mono Creek	131 (779)	6 (33)	1 (9)	Forester Pass - 13,180' Glen Pass - 11,978' Pinchot Pass - 12,130' Mather Pass - 12,100' Muir Pass - 11,955' Selden Pass - 10,900'

[1] The numbers shown in parentheses are the cumulative number of miles and number of days for the entire three summers.
[2] Below Mulkey Pass and off the Pacific Crest Trail.

Week	Dates	Start & End	Mileage	Run Days	Rest Days	Passes, Gaps, and Junctions
7	Aug. 21 thru Aug. 27	Mono Creek to Sonora Pass	141 (920)	5 (38)	2 (11)	Silver Pass - 10,900′ Island Pass - 10,200′ Donohue Pass - 11,056′ Benson Pass - 10,140′ Seavey Pass - 9,150′ Dorothy Lake Pass - 9,550′ Sonora Pass - 9,624′
8	Aug. 28 thru Sept. 3	Sonora Pass to Near Middle Velma Lake	91 (1,011)	5 (43)	2 (13)	Wolf Creek Pass - 8,410′ Ebbetts Pass - 8,700′ Carson Pass - 8,580′ Echo Summit - 7,390′ Dicks Pass - 9,380′
9[1]	Sept. 4 thru Sept. 5	Near Middle Velma Lake to Donner Pass	44 (1,055)	2 (45)	0 (13)	Barker Pass - 7,650′ Donner Pass - 7,090′

---

[1] Partial week.

Summary of '86

Week	Dates	Start & End	Mileage	Run Days	Rest Days	Passes, Gaps, and Junctions
1	July 5 thru July 11	Donner Pass to Bucks Lake Wilderness	116 (1,171)	5 (50)	2 (15)	None
2	July 12 thru July 18	Bucks Lake Wilderness to Big Pine Camp[1]	110 (1,281)	5 (55)	2 (17)	Humboldt Summit - 6,610′
3	July 19 thru July 25	Big Pine Camp to Moosehead Creek	84 (1,365)	4 (59)	3 (20)	Bartle Gap - 5,070′
4	July 26 thru Aug. 1	Moosehead Creek to Carter Meadow	129 (1,494)	5 (64)	2 (22)	Scott Mtn.Summit - 5,401′ Etna Summit - 5,960′
5	Aug. 2 thru Aug. 8	Carter Meadow to Wrangle Gap	120 (1,614)	6 (70)	1 (23)	Cook & Green Pass - 4,770′ Wrangle Gap - 6,496′
6	Aug. 9 thru Aug. 15	Wrangle Gap to Margurette Lake[2]	93 (1,707)	4 (74)	3 (26)	Siskiyou Gap - 5,890′ Grouse Gap - 6,630′
7	Aug. 16 thru Aug. 22	Margurette Lake to Maidu Lake[3]	80 (1,787)	4 (78)	3 (29)	Windigo Pass - 5,820′

[1] Just outside Lassen Volcanic National Park on Pacific Crest Trail alternate.
[2] On Pacific Crest Trail alternate.
[3] Short distance off Pacific Crest Trail.

Week	Dates	Start & End	Mileage	Run Days	Rest Days	Passes, Gaps, and Junctions
8	Aug. 23 thru Aug. 29	Maidu Lake to Lava Lake	134 (1,921)	5 (83)	2 (31)	Scott Pass - 6,040′ McKenzie Pass - 5,280′ Santiam Pass - 4,810′
9	Aug. 30 thru Sept. 5	Lava Lake to Timberline Lodge[1]	120 (2,041)	5 (88)	2 (33)	Red Wolf Pass - 4,120′ Wapinitia Pass - 3,910′ Barlow Pass - 4,161′
10[2]	Sept. 6 thru Sept. 8	Timberline Lodge to Columbia River	54 (2,095)	2 (90)	1 (34)	None

---

[1] Located at Mt. Hood.
[2] Partial week.

Summer of '87

Week	Dates	Start & End	Mileage	Run Days	Rest Days	Passes, Gaps, and Junctions
1	July 22 thru July 28	Columbia River to White Pass	125 (2,220)	5 (95)	2 (36)	Cispus Pass - 6,460' Elk Pass - 6,680' Tieton Pass - 4,570' White Pass - 4,405'
2	July 29 thru Aug. 4	White Pass to Snoqualmie Pass	100 (2,320)	4 (99)	3 (39)	Chinook Pass - 5,432' Sourdough Gap - 6,440' Pickhandle Gap - 6,040' Blue Bell Pass - 6,390' Bullion Pass - 6,479' Scout Pass - 6,530' Hayden Pass - 6,150' Martinsen Gap - 5,720' Rod's Gap - 4,820' Windy Gap - 5,200' Green Pass - 4,940' Tacoma Pass - 3,460' Sheets Pass - 3,720' Stampede Pass - 3,680' Dandy Pass - 3,680' Yakima Pass - 3,575' Snoqualmie Pass - 3,127'
3	Aug. 5 thru Aug. 11	Snoqualmie Pass to Kennedy Hot Spring[1]	121 (2,441)	5 (104)	2 (41)	Needle Site Gap - 5,930' Chikamin Pass - 5,780' Cathedral Pass - 5,610' Deception Pass - 4,470' Pieper Pass - 5,920' Trap Pass - 5,800' Stevens Pass - 4,060' Union Gap - 4,700' Wenatchee Pass - 4,230' Saddle Gap - 5,060' Cady Pass - 4,310' Wards Pass - 5,710' Dishpan Gap - 5,600' Indian Pass - 5,020' Lower White Pass - 5,378' White Pass - 5,904' Red Pass - 6,500'

[1] On Pacific Crest Trail alternate.

Week	Dates	Start & End	Mileage	Run Days	Rest Days	Passes, Gaps, and Junctions
4	Aug. 12 thru Aug. 18	Kennedy Hot Spring to Rainy Pass	65 (2,506)	3 (107)	4 (45)	Fire Creek Pass - 6,350′ Suiattle Pass - 5,990′ Rainy Pass - 4,855′
5[1]	Aug. 19 thru Aug. 22	Rainy Pass to Monument 78[2]	75 (2,581)	3 (110)	1 (46)	Cutthroat Pass - 6,820′ Granite Pass - 6,290′ Methow Pass - 6,600′ Glacier Pass - 5,520′ Harts Pass - 6,198′ Buffalo Pass - 6,550′ Windy Pass - 6,257′ Foggy Pass - 6,180′ Jim Pass - 6,270′ Holman Pass - 5,050′ Rock Pass - 6,491′ Woody Pass - 6,624′ Hopkins Pass - 6,122′ Castle Pass - 5,451′

---

[1] Partial week.
[2] Canadian border.

Glossary

Abutment Wall or barrier.

Access trail Connects the main trail to other trails, a road, or a town. These trails are critical for resupply.

Anti-inflammatory Drug used to counteract inflammation.

Basin A bowl-shaped depression in the surface of the earth.

Blaze Trail marking. Can be a cut or painted symbol on a tree, a sign, or a cairn.

Box canyon A canyon with no passable route at its head and surrounded by steep sidewalls.

Buckthorn A southern desert shrub with sharp thorns.

Cache Supplies, especially food, hidden near the trail for future use.

Camber The natural, slight convex curve of a trail.

Camp robbers Birds that frequent camp and skilled at stealing your food.

Cairn A constructed mound of rock located adjacent to a trail to mark it in open alpine areas or dry washes.

Chaparral A dense thicket of shrubs or small trees that can survive low rainfall and rapid water runoff.

Clearcut An area in which all trees have been cut.

Contour A line of constant elevation.

Counter-balance A food-hanging system in which two bags of edibles are tied at opposite ends of a rope strung over a tree branch.

Creosote Bush that contains an oily liquid that preserves wood.

Ford A natural stream crossing that has been improved sufficiently for use by horses and humans.

Giardia An infection of the lower intestines caused by an amoebic cyst (giardia lamblia) found in contaminated water. Symptoms include stomach cramps, diarrhea, loss of appetite, and vomiting.

Grade A trail's degree of inclination.

Hostel Inexpensive lodging often offering dormitory-type accommodations.

Ibuprofen Oral anti-inflammatory.

Knob A prominent rounded hill or mountain.

Labiosan	Lip sunburn and fever blister medication.
Micatin	Antifungal itch medication.
Pacer	A friend who runs alongside for company, camaraderie, and safety.
Pass	A narrow gap between mountain peaks.
Piñons	Low growing pines of Western North America with edible seeds.
Potable	Drinkable.
Power hiker	Someone who covers long distances.
Ravine	A deep narrow gouge in the earth's surface.
Runoff	Rainfall not absorbed by the soil.
Saddle	A broad low point between two peaks.
Scree slope	A slope that consists of small rocks and gravel.
Seasonal creek	A creek that flows only during the rainy season.
Side trail	Usually a dead-end path off a main trail; often leads to features that the main trail misses.
Switchback	A zig-zag in a trail up the side of a steep hill or mountain.
Talus slope	A rock-covered slope.
Tarn	A small, lush mountain lake.
Thru-hiker	A person covering a long trail in one continuous trek.
Trailhead	The start of a trail.
Traverse	To go across a slope either level or at a small angle.
Ultramarathoner or Ultrarunner	A person who runs distances greater than a marathon.
Undulating trail	A trail that follows a wave-like course, for example, a trail that crosses a series of gullies.
Wash	An area eroded by moving water.
Waterbar	A rock or log barrier that diverts water off a trail.
Whiteout	The condition of low or no visibility caused by thick clouds over a snow-covered landscape.

References

Pacific Crest Trail

1. Clarke, Clinton C. *The Pacific Crest Trailway*. Pasadena, CA: The Pacific Crest Trail System Conference, 1945.

2. Green, David. *A Pacific Crest Odyssey*. Berkeley, CA: Wilderness Press, 1979.

3. Jardine, Ray. *The Pacific Crest Hiker's Handbook*. LaPine, OR: Adventure Lore Press, 1992.

4. Ross, Cindy. *Journey on the Crest*. Seattle, WA: The Mountaineers, 1987.

5. Schaffer, Jeffrey P., Ben Schifrin, Thomas Winnett, and J.C. Jenkins. *The Pacific Crest Trail, Volume 1: California (4th ed.)*. Berkeley, CA (4th ed.): Wilderness Press, 1989.

6. Schaffer, Jeffrey P., and Andy Selters. *The Pacific Crest Trail, Volume 2: Oregon and Washington (5th ed.)*. Berkeley, CA: Wilderness Press, 1990.

Backpacking and Mountaineering

1. Beckey, Fred. *Cascade Alpine Guide, Climbing & High Routes, Volume 1: Columbia River to Stevens Pass*. Seattle, WA: The Mountaineers, 1974.

2. Beckey, Fred. *Cascade Alpine Guide, Climbing & High Routes, Volume 2: Stevens Pass to Rainy Pass*. Seattle, WA: The Mountaineers, 1978.

3. Darvill, Fred T., M.D. *Mountaineering Medicine (11th ed.)*. Berkeley, CA: Wilderness Press, 1985.

4. Fear, Gene. *Surviving the Unexpected Wilderness Emergency*. Tacoma, WA: Survival Education Association, 1972.

5. Fletcher, Colin. *The Complete Walker III*. New York, NY: Knopf, 1984.

6. Hargrove, Penny, and Noelle Liebrenz. *Backpackers' Sourcebook (3rd ed.)*. Berkeley, CA: Wilderness Press, 1986.

7. Lathrop, Theodore G., M.D. *Hypothermia — Killer of the Unprepared*. Portland, OR: Mazamas, 1975.

8. Linkhart, Luther. *The Trinity Alps, A Hiking and Backpacking Guide*. Berkeley, CA: Wilderness Press, 1986.

9. Manning, Harvey. *Backpacking One Step at a Time (3rd ed.)*. New York, NY: Knopf, 1980.

194 References

10. McPhee, John. *The Control of Nature*. New York, NY: Farrar Straus Giroux, 1989.

11. Muir, John. *My First Summer in the Sierra*. New York, NY: Penguin Books, 1987.

12. Peters, Ed, ed. *Mountaineering — The Freedom of the Hills*. Seattle, WA: The Mountaineers, 1982.

13. Rowell, Galen. *Along the High Wild Sierra — The John Muir Trail*. Washington, D.C. National Geographic, April 1989, pp. 467-493.

14. Schaffer, Jeffrey P. *Crater Lake National Park and Vicinity*. Berkeley, CA: Wilderness Press, 1983.

15. Wilkerson, James A., M.D., ed. *Medicine for Mountaineering (3rd ed.)*. Seattle, WA: The Mountaineers, 1985.

16. Winnett, Thomas. *Backpacking Basics*. Berkeley, CA: Wilderness Press, 1979.

Running and Inspirational

1. Anderson, Bob. *Stretching*. Bolinas, CA: Shelter Publications, Inc., 1980.

2. Benyo, Richard. *The Death Valley 300*. Forestville, CA: Specific Publications, 1991.

3. Gagarin, Peter, Fred Pilon, and Stan Wagon. *UltraRunning Magazine*. Sunderland, MA: Self-Published ten times annually since 1981.

4. Glasser, William. *Positive Addiction*. New York, NY: Harper and Row Publishers, Inc., 1976.

5. Henderson, Joe. *The Long Run Solution*. Mountain View, CA: World Publications, Inc., 1976.

6. Hlavac, Harry. *The Foot Book*. Mountain View, CA: World Publications, Inc., 1979.

7. Irwin, Bill, with David McCasland. *Blind Courage*. Waco, TX: WRS Publishing, 1992.

8. Moore, Kenny. *Best Efforts*. Tallahassee, FL: Cedarwinds, 1982.

9. Reese, Paul and Joe Henderson. Ten Million Steps. Waco, TX: WRS Publishing, 1994.

10. Sheehan, George A., M.D. *Dr. Sheehan on Running*. Mountain View, CA: World Publications, Inc., 1975.

11. Subotnick, Steven I., D.P.S., M.S. *The Running Foot Doctor*. Mountain View, CA: World Publications, Inc., 1977.

12. Wellman, Mark and John Flinn. *Climbing Back*. Waco, TX: WRS Publishing, 1992.